I0520651

THE
COMPASS

A WORKBOOK FOR
OWN THE FUTURE

A Master Guide to
Living, Leading, and Deciding with
Integrity and Impact.

This work brings together the 100 Principles,
their Reflections, and 86 Decision Questions
that guide strategy, alignment, and legacy.

KL RENNER
Founder of FORT Group LLC,
TRIVIX Group LLC, Othralis LLC,
And Mythara Studios LLC

TORCHLINE
PRESS
Published by Torchline Press

TORCHLINE PRESS

Copyright © 2025 by Torchline Media LLC
All rights reserved.

Cover design and Interior design: Othralis LLC
Illustrations: Property of Othralis LLC

No part of this book may be copied, stored in a retrieval system, or transmitted in any form or by any means: electronic, mechanical, photocopying, recording, or otherwise, without the prior written permission of the publisher, except for brief quotations used in critical articles or reviews.

This book is for informational and educational purposes only. The author and publisher are not engaged in rendering legal, tax, investment, or financial advice. The ideas and strategies contained herein may not be suitable for every individual or situation. The reader should consult with a licensed professional where appropriate.

Every effort has been made to ensure the accuracy of the content. However, laws and business practices evolve, and the author makes no representations or warranties about the accuracy, applicability, or completeness of the content in this book. The author and publisher disclaim any liability, loss, or risk incurred as a consequence, directly or indirectly, from the use and application of any of the contents of this work.

Names and identifying details may have been changed to protect privacy.

Paperback ISBN: 979-8-9995582-5-1
1st Edition October 2025
Printed in the United States of America.

Published in the United States by: Torchline Press
an imprint of Torchline Media LLC
www.TorchlinePress.com
KL Renner is a pen name of Jeremy L. Christensen
Torchline Press and the Torchline mark are trademarks of Torchline Media LLC.

AI & Machine Learning Notice:
This book, its structure, contents, and language are protected under copyright law. No portion of this work, in any form, may be used in the training, fine-tuning, ingestion, or processing by artificial intelligence or machine learning systems, including large language models (LLMs), without the express written consent of the copyright holder.

TABLE OF CONTENTS

PREFACE

A LETTER FROM THE AUTHOR

Dear Reader,

This is not a book to skim, finish, and forget.
It was never written for the shelf. It was built for the road.

'Own The Future' gave you the vision. It laid out the philosophy, the framework, the larger map of what's possible. But vision without direction is a dream. That's why I wrote 'The Compass'. This isn't a collection of slogans. It is the instrument I carry myself. The system I've tested in the boardroom, in hard conversations, in moments of risk and loss, in hours when no one else was looking.

What you hold in your hands is meant to be used. Written in. Wrestled with. Opened and returned to whenever the noise gets too loud, or the path ahead gets clouded.

Inside you'll find the 100 principles I live by. The reflections that explain not just what they are, but why they matter. The questions I ask myself when the pressure rises and the easy answer won't do.

These are not theories. They are scars, lessons, and field notes. They were earned the long way, through repetition and failure, through building, leading, and rebuilding again. And my hope is that they don't just guide you, but that they provoke you, push you to face your misalignments, to see clearly where you've been drifting, and to step back into alignment with who you've committed to become.

I'll say this plainly: life will not slow down for you. Markets will shift. People will disappoint you. Pressure will find you. But truth doesn't move. And if your direction doesn't align with it, don't move.

This Compass will not make your journey easy. But it will make it clear. It will not promise perfection. But it will help you choose alignment over distraction, signal over noise, direction over speed.

Carry it. Use it. Test it against your reality. That's when it comes alive.

Your future is not waiting to be discovered, it is waiting to be built. And this is the tool I've built to help you own it.

With you on the path,

- KL Renner

Section I

The Principles That Govern Everything

The Pages of Principles

These are not just beliefs. They are architecture, the foundation beneath how I live, lead, build, and serve in business and in life.

They began as convictions. Over time, they hardened into code.

Each principle is more than a phrase. It is a framework, tested in risk, refined by repetition, and proven under pressure. They are how I decide what to build, who to trust, when to move, and what to protect.

What follows is the complete, unfiltered collection. You'll see the principle itself, why it matters, how it functions, and the outcomes it drives. Together, they form a compass; a living alignment mechanism I return to again and again.

Because the terrain will change. Markets will shift. The noise will rise. But these? These stay true.

If it doesn't align with these principles, I don't move.

1. **Ownership Is the Only Leverage That Lasts**
   Control the outcome, or be controlled by it. Ownership isn't just about equity. It's about responsibility. About being the final name on the line. I don't chase applause or short-term wins, I chase control.

   Why it matters: If I don't own it, I don't control it. Ownership brings freedom.
   How it helps: I stay accountable, and every move builds equity.
   Outcome: No one else can cancel or cut me out, I own the upside.

2. **Move First. Move Fast. Don't Wait for Permission.**
   Speed is a weapon. So is initiative. I make the first move. I create the future others have to adapt to.

   Why it matters: The window is rarely open for long.
   How it helps: I act on instinct before analysis kills momentum.
   Outcome: I set the pace, create opportunity, and leave hesitation behind.

3. **Build Systems, Not Just Goals**
   Goals are wishes. Systems are weapons. I design frameworks that force momentum and remove friction.

   Why it matters: Goals fail without structure.
   How it helps: I build systems that remove willpower from the equation.
   Outcome: Discipline becomes automatic. Outcomes become inevitable.

4. Play Wealth Games, Not Status Games

I don't chase clout. I chase freedom. Time, deal flow, and ownership mean more than attention.

Why it matters: Status fades. Wealth compounds.
How it helps: I chase freedom, not validation.
Outcome: I build leverage, not optics.

5. Protect the Signal. Eliminate the Noise.

Focus is currency. I protect my attention like a billion-dollar asset. I say no more than I say yes.

Why it matters: Distraction is the death of vision.
How it helps: I curate inputs, people, and focus zones.
Outcome: My clarity grows. My results sharpen.

6. Play Long-Term Games with Long-Term People

I build with people I trust. If we can't run for a decade together, we won't run for a day.

Why it matters: Trust compounds like capital.
How it helps: I invest in aligned relationships that multiply over time.
Outcome: I build teams, not transactions.

7. Wealth Without Purpose Is Poverty in Disguise

Money is a multiplier. With purpose, it fuels transformation. Without it, it multiplies insecurity.

Why it matters: Without purpose, money becomes a prison.
How it helps: I tie my income to impact.
Outcome: I stay fulfilled, not just paid.

8. Strategy Over Emotion

I act based on leverage and logic, not on fear, pride, or urgency.

Why it matters: Emotion is fuel. Strategy is steering.
How it helps: I feel, but I don't flinch.
Outcome: I stay effective when others panic.

9. Burn the Old Maps

I don't follow paths made for someone else. I create new terrain.

Why it matters: Old paths lead to old destinations.
How it helps: I design from first principles, not tradition.
Outcome: I build new categories, not recycled careers.

10. **Be Dangerous, But Disciplined**
Power must be guided. I stay sharp, but I wield it with care.

Why it matters: Strength without discipline destroys.
How it helps: I stay calm, collected, and capable.
Outcome: I become trusted under pressure.

11. **Build for Impact, Not Just Income**
If it doesn't echo after I'm gone, it wasn't big enough.

Why it matters: The world doesn't need more noise. It needs transformation.
How it helps: I prioritize depth over width.
Outcome: My work becomes legacy, not just commerce.

12. **Never Outsource the Final Decision**
Advice is welcome. But the weight is mine. I decide.

Why it matters: I live with the outcome. So I make the call.
How it helps: I listen, then I lead.
Outcome: I take ownership of both wins and losses.

13. **Find the Signal in Suffering**
Pain is a teacher. I don't waste it. I transmute it.

Why it matters: Pain clarifies what matters.
How it helps: I ask better questions when things fall apart.
Outcome: I use hardship as raw material for growth.

14. **Integrity Is the Real Infinite Cheat Code**
Truth compounds. Lies subtract. I play long, and I play clean.

Why it matters: Truth scales. Lies collapse.
How it helps: I earn trust without trying.
Outcome: I never have to look over my shoulder.

15. **Build What Outlasts You**
Not just to succeed, but to leave something that doesn't need me to keep running.

Why it matters: My time is finite. My impact doesn't have to be.
How it helps: I build legacy infrastructure.
Outcome: I create something others will inherit.

16. **If the Game Is Rigged, Change the Game**
I don't ask to be let in. I build the door. I write the rules.

Why it matters: The system was never built for me. So I build better systems.
How it helps: I stop begging and start building.
Outcome: I become the gatekeeper.

17. Your Name Is a Contract
When I put my name on something, it becomes a reflection of who I am.

Why it matters: Every signature is a reflection.
How it helps: I only commit to what I can honor.
Outcome: My name earns compound respect.

18. Pressure Reveals, It Doesn't Create
I welcome it. I want to know what I'm made of.

Why it matters: Crisis exposes foundation.
How it helps: I welcome the test.
Outcome: I emerge forged, not fragile.

19. Build Moats, Not Just Castles
A shiny win means nothing if it can't be defended.

Why it matters: It's not enough to win. You have to defend it.
How it helps: I design durability into everything.
Outcome: What I build can't be easily copied.

20. Reputation Is Interest on Character
It compounds quietly. I guard it relentlessly.

Why it matters: Image fades. Integrity accrues.
How it helps: I choose consistent principles over performative moments.
Outcome: I earn long-term trust.

21. Serve First. Scale Second.
Value must exist before volume. Transformation before transaction.

Why it matters: Value precedes volume.
How it helps: I earn loyalty by leading with results.
Outcome: My reputation grows before my revenue does.

22. Scarcity Is a Signal
If everyone is doing it, it's probably not worth doing. I go where others haven't.

Why it matters: The crowd is often wrong.
How it helps: I go where others aren't looking.
Outcome: I find untapped leverage and uncommon opportunity.

23. Hire for Alignment First
Skills can be taught. Values can't.

Why it matters: Skill without integrity is dangerous.
How it helps: I build teams on shared values.
Outcome: Culture protects performance.

24. Proximity Is Power

I curate my circle. If I wouldn't trade places with someone, I don't take advice from them.

Why it matters: Who I'm around shapes what I believe is possible.
How it helps: I choose rooms that stretch me.
Outcome: I elevate faster and normalize excellence.

25. Complexity Is a Sign of Poor Design

Simplicity is strength. The more elegant the system, the more powerful the result.

Why it matters: Confusion costs momentum.
How it helps: I strip away what doesn't matter.
Outcome: Simplicity makes execution seamless.

26. Don't Just Learn. Integrate.

Knowledge is noise until it becomes embodied.

Why it matters: Information without application is noise.
How it helps: I apply what I know immediately.
Outcome: I move from knowledge to transformation.

27. Leverage Everything

Capital. Attention. Talent. Time. I look for asymmetric upside in every situation.

Why it matters: My time and energy are finite.
How it helps: I look for asymmetric returns.
Outcome: Small inputs lead to outsized gains.

28. Feedback Is a Weapon

Even when it cuts, I collect it. I want to see the blind spots.

Why it matters: Blind spots are expensive.
How it helps: I collect insight even when it stings.
Outcome: I grow faster and lead better.

29. Crisis Is a Growth Curve in Disguise

When everything breaks, it reveals where the real work needs to happen.

Why it matters: Challenge is a mirror.
How it helps: I let the fire forge me.
Outcome: I evolve through adversity.

30. Be the Client You Wish to Serve

I model the behavior I expect. I lead from the inside.

Why it matters: I model what I expect.
How it helps: I attract who I reflect.
Outcome: I magnetize ideal partnerships.

31. Master the Boring Stuff

Repetition. Discipline. Diligence. These are the quiet engines behind every great story.

Why it matters: Success hides in repetition.
How it helps: I find pride in precision.
Outcome: Excellence becomes automatic.

32. Volume Before Precision

Start messy. Start loud. Perfection is a reward, not a prerequisite.

Why it matters: Perfection delays progress.
How it helps: I ship early, then improve.
Outcome: I learn faster and iterate smarter.

33. Learn in Public

I share the climb. It attracts those on a similar path.

Why it matters: Transparency invites trust.
How it helps: I attract community through authenticity.
Outcome: I grow through feedback and accountability.

34. Say Less, Mean More

Clarity is power. Brevity is strength.

Why it matters: Words are currency.
How it helps: I cut through noise with clarity.
Outcome: My message lands harder.

35. Build the Brand Before You Need It

Reputation isn't a rescue rope. It's a runway.

Why it matters: Reputation is earned in the quiet seasons.
How it helps: I invest early in identity.
Outcome: Opportunity finds me before I go looking.

36. Borrow Belief Until Yours Is Built

I move forward, even if all I have is faith in the process.

Why it matters: Confidence can be constructed.
How it helps: I move forward even when I'm unsure.
Outcome: Action builds certainty.

37. Your Energy Introduces You Before You Speak

I manage presence like a resource. I don't spill it casually.

Why it matters: Presence creates perception.
How it helps: I lead with congruence and conviction.
Outcome: People feel my clarity before I explain it.

38. No One Is Coming. Build It Anyway.
Entitlement kills momentum. I take the next step.

Why it matters: Waiting is wasted time.
How it helps: I take the first step.
Outcome: I create momentum others can join.

39. The Best Deal Is the One You Can Walk Away From
Freedom is the ability to say no without flinching.

Why it matters: Neediness kills negotiation.
How it helps: I hold boundaries with calm power.
Outcome: I win from a position of strength.

40. Don't Scale What You Haven't Proven
Growth amplifies flaws. I perfect the model first.

Why it matters: Amplifying broken systems breaks everything.
How it helps: I validate before I expand.
Outcome: I scale what's solid.

41. If It's Not Written, It's Not Real
Ideas live on paper. Execution lives on a plan.

Why it matters: Memory is fragile. Documentation endures.
How it helps: I clarify and commit through writing.
Outcome: My vision becomes actionable and trackable.

42. What You Tolerate, You Teach
I lead by what I allow. Standards are non-negotiable.

Why it matters: Standards don't enforce themselves.
How it helps: I lead with consistency, not contradiction.
Outcome: I build cultures of clarity and strength.

43. Rest Is a Weapon, Not a Weakness
Recovery is part of resilience. I protect my margins.

Why it matters: Burnout doesn't build anything sustainable.
How it helps: I recharge with intention.
Outcome: I stay resilient for the long game.

44. Urgency Without Direction Is Chaos
I move with intensity, but always with aim.

Why it matters: Hustle means nothing without aim.
How it helps: I align speed with purpose.
Outcome: I produce precision, not panic.

45. Keep the Sword Sharp, Even in Peace

I prepare before the storm. The best time to train is when you don't have to.

Why it matters: Calm seasons are for preparation.
How it helps: I train before it's needed.
Outcome: I'm ready when it counts.

46. What You Build Builds You

Every project sculpts my character. I choose wisely.

Why it matters: Work doesn't just shape outcomes, it shapes identity.
How it helps: I build projects that refine me.
Outcome: I evolve with every creation.

47. Work Ethic Wins When Talent Rests

I don't coast. I compound.

Why it matters: Talent is common. Discipline isn't.
How it helps: I outlast with consistency.
Outcome: I win by showing up when others stop.

48. Mastery Is Bought in Boredom

The repetitions no one sees are the ones that matter most.

Why it matters: Repetition is the furnace of greatness.
How it helps: I train beyond the point where others quit.
Outcome: Mastery becomes muscle memory.

49. Celebrate Quiet Wins

Not everything needs applause. Progress is its own reward.

Why it matters: Progress without applause still matters.
How it helps: I validate effort, not just outcomes.
Outcome: I stay grateful and grounded.

50. Stay Hungry. Stay Humble. Stay Building.

The climb never ends. Neither does the calling.

Why it matters: Success can dull the edge.
How it helps: I remain a student and a builder.
Outcome: I keep growing, regardless of external praise.

51. Never Let Ego Close a Door That Humility Could Open

Pride can cost partnerships. I choose growth over ego.

Why it matters: Pride is expensive.
How it helps: I stay open to correction, collaboration, and course change.
Outcome: I keep options open and allies close.

52. Build Wealth That Can't Be Measured in Dollars

Trust, loyalty, peace of mind. These are the real assets.

Why it matters: Peace, love, and time are the real assets.
How it helps: I prioritize relationships and internal harmony.
Outcome: I live rich, not just look rich.

53. Make It Easy to Say Yes

Clarity, value, and timing beat persuasion every time.

Why it matters: Friction kills momentum.
How it helps: I bring clarity, timing, and value.
Outcome: I close faster and build better partnerships.

54. Don't Just Solve Problems. Eliminate Them at the Root.

I don't put out fires. I redesign the building.

Why it matters: Band-aids create bigger messes.
How it helps: I find the cause, not just the symptom.
Outcome: I prevent repeat chaos.

55. Power Is Best Used Quietly

The strongest move often doesn't need an audience.

Why it matters: Loud leaders leak trust.
How it helps: I let action be the amplifier.
Outcome: I become someone others trust instinctively.

56. Protect the Asymmetry

I spend hours on what gives me 10x back. Most people never do.

Why it matters: Not all ROI is equal.
How it helps: I guard time, focus, and decisions that yield outsized gains.
Outcome: I multiply outcomes while reducing input.

57. Design for Scale, Operate with Intimacy

Even as I grow, I stay close to the signal.

Why it matters: Scale shouldn't sacrifice soul.
How it helps: I keep the human layer alive as I grow.
Outcome: My growth feels personal, not transactional.

58. Stop Explaining to People Who Don't Want to Understand

I protect my energy from unqualified opinions.

Why it matters: Misunderstood energy is wasted energy.
How it helps: I invest my clarity in people who are ready.
Outcome: I lead with focus, not frustration.

59. Make Your Absence Felt, Not Your Presence Tolerated
Value is measured in impact, not noise.

Why it matters: Legacy is measured by impact, not attendance.
How it helps: I contribute in ways that outlast meetings.
Outcome: I become essential without needing the spotlight.

60. Confidence Comes from Evidence
I build belief by keeping promises to myself.

Why it matters: Belief must be built, not borrowed.
How it helps: I stack wins and keep promises to myself.
Outcome: I walk in earned conviction.

61. Show Up Ready, Not Needy
I come with something to offer, not something to beg for.

Why it matters: Desperation dilutes influence.
How it helps: I bring solutions, not needs.
Outcome: I negotiate from power.

62. Operate Like It's Already Yours
Ownership is a mindset long before it's a title.

Why it matters: Mindset precedes results.
How it helps: I carry ownership energy into every room.
Outcome: I'm treated like I already belong.

63. Let the Work Speak So Loud They Forget to Ask for Credentials
I don't explain. I deliver.

Why it matters: Results silence doubt.
How it helps: I overdeliver instead of overselling.
Outcome: My work earns more respect than my title.

64. Learn Fast. Adjust Faster.
Speed of adaptation is survival. I don't fear being wrong, I fear being stuck.

Why it matters: Slow learners get left behind.
How it helps: I update my beliefs and models in real time.
Outcome: I stay relevant and resilient.

65. Build on First Principles, Not Trends
Trends fade. Truth compounds. I build from the bedrock.

Why it matters: Noise fades. Fundamentals last.
How it helps: I anchor in timeless logic.
Outcome: I build things that endure.

66. **Fight for Simplicity**
    The more powerful the idea, the simpler its delivery. Complexity hides weakness.

    Why it matters: Complexity is a mask.
    How it helps: I keep things clean, lean, and actionable.
    Outcome: Execution accelerates.

67. **Practice Loud, So You Can Perform Quiet**
    I train in public. I deliver in silence. Mastery makes the loud things effortless.

    Why it matters: Training prepares the subconscious.
    How it helps: I work publicly and unglamorously.
    Outcome: I perform naturally under pressure.

68. **Seek Friction That Sharpens, Not Drains**
    I welcome challenge from those who want me better, not bitter.

    Why it matters: Conflict can create clarity.
    How it helps: I invite feedback from people who want me to win.
    Outcome: I refine without resentment.

69. **Don't Aim to Be Liked. Aim to Be Respected.**
    If I must choose, I choose truth over approval.

    Why it matters: Approval fades. Respect sticks.
    How it helps: I lead from conviction, not consensus.
    Outcome: I attract what I stand for.

70. **Be the One Who Calls It First**
    The visionary always sounds crazy, until they're proven right.

    Why it matters: Visionaries lead the wave.
    How it helps: I speak my insight before it's safe.
    Outcome: I create trend, not follow it.

71. **Grow the Roots Before You Show the Leaves**
    I build depth before show. Quiet foundation, loud results.

    Why it matters: Foundation beats flash.
    How it helps: I build depth before display.
    Outcome: I scale with stability.

72. **Know the Difference Between Urgent and Important**
    I prioritize what compounds, not just what screams.

    Why it matters: Urgency steals attention.
    How it helps: I filter noise from signal.
    Outcome: I get the right things done.

73. Study Outcomes, Not Opinions
I look at results, not noise, narratives, or feelings.

Why it matters: Most opinions aren't paid for.
How it helps: I look at results, not rhetoric.
Outcome: I copy what works, not what's loud.

74. Use Money to Buy Time, Not Just Things
The highest ROI is time reclaimed for what matters.

Why it matters: Time is the rarest asset.
How it helps: I invest in leverage and peace.
Outcome: I live on my own schedule.

75. Stop Playing Defense with Your Life
I don't just react. I impose direction.

Why it matters: Reaction limits potential.
How it helps: I design a proactive strategy.
Outcome: I own my outcomes.

76. Don't Water What Won't Grow
Some ideas, people, and seasons are meant to be outgrown.

Why it matters: Energy is finite.
How it helps: I let go of deadweight.
Outcome: I cultivate what actually multiplies.

77. Become Impossible to Replace
I aim to be the person the mission can't afford to lose.

Why it matters: Irreplaceability is job security.
How it helps: I do what only I can do, better than anyone else.
Outcome: I build unshakable leverage.

78. Build Trust Before You Ask for It
Every action is a deposit. Trust is earned through consistency.

Why it matters: Trust is earned, not assumed.
How it helps: I show up consistently before I ask for commitment.
Outcome: People say yes because they believe me.

79. Craft Offers That Sell Themselves
I design value so clear it doesn't need convincing.

Why it matters: Obvious value doesn't need pressure.
How it helps: I stack proof, clarity, and urgency.
Outcome: Conversions happen naturally.

80. Let the Right Things Take Time

Not everything is meant to scale fast. Some things are worth building slowly.

Why it matters: Good things grow slow.
How it helps: I stay patient where it matters.
Outcome: I build things that last.

81. Audit for Alignment Often

I don't just ask "is it working?," I ask "is it still right?"

Why it matters: Misalignment compounds.
How it helps: I check goals, people, and systems regularly.
Outcome: I don't drift. I adjust.

82. Learn to Leave Before You Break

Not all exits are failures. Some are a form of wisdom.

Why it matters: Wisdom exits early.
How it helps: I leave at peak, not collapse.
Outcome: I pivot with grace, not regret.

83. Build Culture Before You Build Company

A toxic team ruins the best ideas. I build from character.

Why it matters: Culture scales or sinks everything.
How it helps: I embed values before systems.
Outcome: I grow with soul, not just structure.

84. Don't Confuse Visibility with Value

Not all that's seen is significant. And not all that matters is on stage.

Why it matters: Loud doesn't equal impactful.
How it helps: I focus on transformation, not trend.
Outcome: I become known for what actually works.

85. Buy Back Your Energy

I delegate, automate, and eliminate so I can do what only I can do.

Why it matters: Energy is the limit.
How it helps: I cut what drains and double down on what drives.
Outcome: I stay energized and effective.

86. Make Your Mission Bigger Than Your Mood

Discipline moves even when motivation doesn't.

Why it matters: Emotion is volatile.
How it helps: I commit to purpose, not convenience.
Outcome: I remain consistent, even on hard days.

87. **Become Known for Something Clear**
    I narrow until I'm undeniable.

    Why it matters: Confused brands get ignored.
    How it helps: I specialize, then dominate.
    Outcome: I become the obvious choice.

88. **Create Outcomes, Not Activity**
    I measure by impact, not busyness.

    Why it matters: Motion isn't progress.
    How it helps: I track impact, not busyness.
    Outcome: I move the needle.

89. **Exit Loops That No Longer Serve You**
    Even good habits can become cages. I evolve intentionally.

    Why it matters: Familiarity isn't freedom.
    How it helps: I cut cycles that cost peace.
    Outcome: I evolve without apology.

90. **Leave Everything Better Than You Found It**
    Whether a meeting, a partnership, or a stranger, I leave a mark.

    Why it matters: Contribution creates legacy.
    How it helps: I lead with value, not ego.
    Outcome: I earn goodwill everywhere I go.

91. **Obsess Over the Details That Matter**
    I don't sweat everything, just the right things.

    Why it matters: Excellence hides in nuance.
    How it helps: I sweat the right stuff.
    Outcome: I build beauty and trust.

92. **Protect the Downside. Then Swing Big.**
    I de-risk ruthlessly so I can go all in when it counts.

    Why it matters: Risk without protection is roulette.
    How it helps: I hedge intelligently, then go all in.
    Outcome: I take bold shots without reckless risk.

93. **Let Data Inform You: But Don't Let It Define You**
    I trust the numbers, but I move with instinct, too.

    Why it matters: Intuition plus insight wins.
    How it helps: I balance gut and graph.
    Outcome: I act faster and smarter.

94. Know the Cost of Saying Yes

Every yes is a no to something else. I spend my focus wisely.

Why it matters: Every yes has a price.
How it helps: I calculate opportunity cost.
Outcome: I protect my priorities.

95. Operate Like a Founder, Even When You're Not

I treat every job, project, and opportunity like my name's on it.

Why it matters: Ownership is mindset before title.
How it helps: I take extreme responsibility.
Outcome: I earn leadership by behavior.

96. Win Quietly, But Keep Score

I don't brag. But I do track.

Why it matters: Success needs no parade.
How it helps: I track progress without bragging.
Outcome: I stay humble and hungry.

97. Build a Life You Don't Need a Vacation From

Escape isn't the goal. Alignment is.

Why it matters: Escaping isn't living.
How it helps: I align work with values.
Outcome: I find peace in the process.

98. Avoid Anything That Complicates Your Peace

Peace is leverage. I won't trade it for vanity or validation.

Why it matters: Peace is the rarest currency.
How it helps: I cut chaos, even if it's profitable.
Outcome: I gain margin to think and thrive.

99. Be Your Own Safety Net

I don't wait for rescue. I build resilience from the inside out.

Why it matters: Self-reliance scales security.
How it helps: I stack resources, skills, and systems.
Outcome: I stay grounded when others shake.

100. Die With Nothing Left Unknown

When I leave, I leave it all on the field. Every idea. Every gift. Every bit of impact I was meant to give.

Why it matters: Potential unused is purpose wasted.
How it helps: I create, share, build, and give until the end.
Outcome: I leave nothing on the table, and no one wondering what I could've been.

REFLECTIONS ON THE PAGES OF PRINCIPLES

WHY I BELIEVE THEM.
HOW THEY WORK.
WHAT THEY UNLOCK.

These are more than phrases. They are patterns. Behaviors I return to when the noise rises. Mental models that simplify complex choices. Spiritual anchors that keep me steady. Decision frameworks that trade impulse for intention.

This section is the bridge between belief and behavior. It explains the reasoning behind each principle, the mechanics that make it effective, and the outcomes it produces when lived over time. It is not theory for theory's sake. It is a field manual: formed by experiments, mistakes, wins, and the quiet repetitions that nobody sees but everyone feels in the results.

What follows is a deep dive into why these principles matter to me, how they've shaped real outcomes, and how they move me toward the only goals that actually matter: peace, purpose, mastery, freedom, legacy, and alignment.

What These Reflections Are
- Context: The story behind the principle and the problem it solves.
- Clarity: A simple model you can remember under pressure.
- Consequence: What happens when you apply it, and when you don't.
- Practice: Prompts, filters, and actions to turn insight into habit.

How To Use This Section
- Work one principle at a time. Depth beats speed. Let a single idea rewire a week.
- Do the exercises. The questions aren't filler; they're the conversion layer from knowing to becoming.
- Track evidence. Confidence is built by kept promises. Record the small wins.
- Return often. New seasons reveal new angles. The same principle will read differently at different levels.

What You'll Notice As You Go
- Patterns emerge. Ownership shows up everywhere. So does integrity. Simplicity. Alignment. They weave together.
- Tradeoffs become obvious. Every "yes" has a cost. Every shortcut has a bill. The reflections help you see the price tag early.
- Your questions improve. Instead of "What should I do?," you begin asking, "What decision keeps me aligned and compounding?"
- Peace increases. Clarity reduces noise. Boundaries get stronger. Energy returns to the work that matters.

What This Is Not
- Motivation. Motivation fades. This is architecture.
- Slogans. If a line can't survive pressure, it doesn't live here.
- A Script. You are not meant to copy my life: only the alignment that makes a life work.

The Six Aims Beneath Every Principle
- Peace: Decisions that protect margin, reduce chaos, and let you think.
- Purpose: Work aligned with calling, not just calendar.
- Mastery: Skill compounded through repetition, feedback, and patience.
- Freedom: Options earned by ownership, systems, and discipline.
- Legacy: Impact designed to outlast you.
- Alignment: Integrity between values, vision, and daily behavior.

A NOTE ON HONESTY

Some reflections will affirm what you're already doing. Others will confront what you've excused. Let them. Alignment is not comfortable, it is clean.

Honesty with yourself is the hardest honesty of all. It asks you to look past the image you project, past the story you tell others, past even the story you've convinced yourself to believe. It requires you to face where you've been drifting, where you've been cutting corners, where you've settled for less than what you said you wanted.

And that will sting.

But the sting is proof that truth is doing its work.

If a principle exposes drift, treat it as a gift, not a threat.

Drift is natural; denial is optional.

Every pilot corrects their course dozens of times in a single flight, not because they are weak, but because correction is strength.

So do not waste energy defending your drift.

Use your energy to realign.

Because alignment is not about shame.

It is about freedom.

Every time you admit what's off and bring it back into line, you take back power. You feel it in your body, in your calendar, in your words. You feel your life get quieter, stronger, and truer.

And that's the test: not whether the work feels easy, but whether it feels clean. Clean decisions, clean motives, clean direction. That kind of honesty won't always make you comfortable, but it will always make you clear.

So turn the page.

Pick a principle.

Do the work.

If it affirms you, stand taller.

If it confronts you, lean in.

If it wounds your pride, let it heal your path.

The leaves will show.

The roots will hold.

And with every correction, your compass will point more faithfully north.

SECTION II

LIVING THE COMPASS

The Principles are the laws.

But laws don't change you unless you live them.

Rules written on a page don't transform a life. They only transform when they become the way you think, the lens you look through, and the line you refuse to cross.

This section is where the Compass shifts from ideas into action, where words move off the paper and into the patterns of your decisions.

Here, each principle is expanded, unpacked with its deeper reasoning, its real-world consequences, and the tools to apply it in your own life. No abstractions, no vague inspiration, just clear tested frameworks designed to move you from knowing to doing.

Every Reflection Includes:

- The Core Idea: the essence of the principle in plain words.
- Why It Matters: the leverage it creates and the cost if ignored.
- How It Helps: the practical way it works when applied.
- The Outcome: what it produces when lived with consistency.
- Reflection Questions: prompts to wrestle with in your own context.
- Workbook Exercises: structured steps to translate principle into practice.
- Decision Filters: selected questions that protect alignment.
- Action Box: a place to commit to a next step, now.

But remember this: the goal is not to master all 100 principles at once.

That is a trap, one that turns clarity into pressure and direction into noise.

The true goal is much simpler: to take one principle at a time, live it, wrestle with it, and let it do its work in the season that matters most.

Some will challenge you immediately. Others will wait quietly until the right moment, when pressure or opportunity calls them forward.

As you move through this section, let the reflections challenge you, guide you, and expose where your alignment is strongest… and where it is drifting.

This is not about comfort.

It is about clarity.

It is not about volume.

It is about precision.

A single principle, lived fully, can reroute an entire life.

These are not theories.

They are alignment mechanisms.

They are how conviction becomes clarity.

How clarity becomes courage.

And how courage, lived daily, becomes legacy.

So approach this section slowly.

Engage with honesty.

Write in the margins.

Stop when something grips you, and don't move on until you've wrestled with it fully.

Because the point is not how quickly you finish these pages, it is how deeply these pages finish their work in you.

PRINCIPLE #1

OWNERSHIP IS THE ONLY LEVERAGE THAT LASTS

The Core Idea:
Control the outcome, or be controlled by it. Ownership isn't just equity, it's responsibility. It means being the final name on the line.

Why It Matters:
If I don't own it, I don't control it. Ownership brings freedom. Without it, I'm renting my future.

How It Helps:
Ownership forces accountability and creates compounding equity; in wealth, reputation, relationships, and legacy.

The Outcome:
No one else can cancel me, cut me out, or cap my upside. I own the reward because I own the risk.

Reflection

Where in my life or business am I still "renting" instead of owning?

Have I taken full responsibility for outcomes, or am I still blaming circumstances/people?

What would change if I decided everything I touch carries my name?

WORKBOOK EXERCISE: OWNERSHIP AUDIT

Step 1: List three key areas of your life (e.g., business, health, relationships).
Business →
Health →
Relationships →

Step 2: For each area, ask:
Do I truly own the outcome here, or am I depending on someone else's decision, approval, or permission?

What would full ownership look like?

Step 3: Write your "Ownership Move" for each area.

Business → (e.g., formalize equity, stop outsourcing final calls)

Health → (e.g., create my own system, stop blaming time)

Relationships → (e.g., take responsibility for communication, stop waiting for others to fix it)

Decision Filter Questions

Does this create ownership or dependency?

Am I saying yes because I want to, or because I'm afraid to say no?

Would I still choose this if no one ever found out I did it?

This Week, I Will Take Ownership Of:

PRINCIPLE #2

MOVE FIRST. MOVE FAST. DON'T WAIT FOR PERMISSION

The Core Idea:
Speed is a weapon. So is initiative. I move first and set the pace before hesitation or doubt can slow me down.

Why It Matters:
Opportunities are fleeting. If I wait for approval, the moment passes and the leverage is gone.

How It Helps:
By acting first, I gain position, momentum, and control. I create the future others are forced to adapt to.

The Outcome:
I seize ground while others are still deciding, and momentum compounds in my favor.

Reflection

Where am I waiting for permission that I don't actually need?

What advantage have I lost in the past because I hesitated?

How would momentum in my life or business shift if I acted as soon as clarity struck?

WORKBOOK EXERCISE: FIRST-MOVE ADVANTAGE

Step 1: List three areas where moving first would create leverage (e.g., business, health, relationships).

Business →
Health →
Relationships →

Step 2: For each area, ask:
What does moving first look like here?

What is the cost of waiting?

Step 3: Write your "First Move" for each area.

Business → (e.g., send the proposal today, launch the pilot, make the call before competitors)

Health → (e.g., start the workout now, book the appointment, commit to the plan today)

Relationships → (e.g., initiate the conversation, extend the invitation, resolve the conflict first)

Decision Filter Questions

Does this action give me a first-move advantage?
Am I moving with clarity or just reacting to pressure?
Is hesitation here protecting me or holding me back?

This Week, I Will Move First On:

PRINCIPLE #3

BUILD SYSTEMS, NOT JUST GOALS

The Core Idea:
Goals are wishes. Systems are weapons. I design frameworks that force momentum and remove friction.

Why It Matters:
Goals without structure collapse under pressure. Systems create consistency that makes outcomes inevitable.

How It Helps:
I build frameworks that replace willpower with design. The system carries me even when motivation fades.

The Outcome:
Discipline becomes automatic. Progress compounds. Results become predictable.

Reflection

Where in my life do I rely on goals without supportive systems?

What routines or structures could replace my reliance on motivation alone?

How would outcomes change if systems guaranteed progress instead of hope?

WORKBOOK EXERCISE: SYSTEM BUILDER

Step 1: Identify three goals you currently have.
Business →
Health →
Personal →

Step 2: For each goal, ask:
What daily or weekly system would make progress automatic?

How can I design friction out of the process?

Step 3: Write your "System Shift" for each area.

Business → (e.g., daily outreach targets, automated workflows, recurring review sessions)

Health → (e.g., scheduled workouts, meal prep routines, sleep schedule)

Personal → (e.g., blocked reading time, family rituals, creative practice)

Decision Filter Questions

Does this create a repeatable system or just a one-time goal?
Am I relying on discipline, or have I designed structure?
Will this process still work when my motivation drops?

This Week, I Will Replace One Goal With A System By:

PRINCIPLE #4

PLAY WEALTH GAMES, NOT STATUS GAMES

The Core Idea:
I don't chase clout. I chase freedom. Time, deal flow, and ownership matter more than attention.

Why It Matters:
Status fades quickly. Wealth, when built with intention, compounds into freedom and long-term leverage.

How It Helps:
I focus on assets, equity, and compounding value instead of optics or validation.

The Outcome:
I build real leverage, not just the appearance of success.

Reflection

Where in my life am I pursuing recognition instead of results?

How much energy am I spending on looking successful versus building freedom?

What choices would shift me from chasing attention to compounding assets?

WORKBOOK EXERCISE: WEALTH VS. STATUS AUDIT

Step 1: List three current pursuits or projects.
Business →
Financial →
Personal →

Step 2: For each, ask:
Am I pursuing this for freedom or for validation?

Does this compound into wealth or fade as status?

Step 3: Write your "Wealth Shift" for each area.
Business → (e.g., invest in equity instead of brand optics)

Financial → (e.g., acquire assets instead of luxury items)

Personal → (e.g., spend time on skills that compound, not just appearances)

Decision Filter Questions

Does this create wealth or just the image of success?
If no one could see it, would I still pursue it?
Will this compound over time, or vanish when the spotlight moves?

This Week, I Will Shift My Focus From Status To Wealth By:

PRINCIPLE #5

PROTECT THE SIGNAL. ELIMINATE THE NOISE

The Core Idea:
Focus is currency. I protect my attention like a billion-dollar asset. I say no more often than I say yes.

Why It Matters:
Distraction is the enemy of vision. Noise consumes clarity, energy, and momentum.

How It Helps:
By curating inputs, people, and environments, I amplify what matters and silence what doesn't.

The Outcome:
My clarity sharpens, execution improves, and results multiply.

Reflection

Where am I allowing noise to drown out signal in my life or work?

What distractions feel urgent but deliver no real value?

How would my results change if I defended my focus as my most valuable resource?

WORKBOOK EXERCISE: SIGNAL VS. NOISE AUDIT

Step 1: List three areas where distraction often steals your attention.
Work →
Technology →
Relationships →

Step 2: For each area, ask:
What is the true signal here?

What noise can be cut, delegated, or eliminated?

Step 3: Write your "Focus Move" for each area.

Work → (e.g., batch emails, block deep work time, eliminate low-value meetings)

Technology → (e.g., delete draining apps, silence non-essential notifications)

Relationships → (e.g., limit toxic conversations, prioritize energizing connections)

Decision Filter Questions

Does this sharpen my focus or scatter it?
Is this a signal worth amplifying, or noise to eliminate?
If I say yes here, what signal will I be forced to say no to?

This Week, I Will Protect My Signal By:

PRINCIPLE #6

PLAY LONG-TERM GAMES WITH LONG-TERM PEOPLE

The Core Idea:
I build with people I trust. If we can't run for a decade together, we won't run for a day.

Why It Matters:
Trust compounds like capital. Partnerships built on alignment last; short-term deals collapse.

How It Helps:
By investing in relationships that share values and vision, I multiply opportunities over time.

The Outcome:
I build teams, not transactions.

Reflection

Who in my life or business has proven they are long-term aligned?

Where am I relying on people who may not last the distance?

What would change if I only partnered with people I trust for the long run?

WORKBOOK EXERCISE: RELATIONSHIP ALIGNMENT AUDIT

Step 1: List three key partnerships or relationships.
Partnership 1 →
Partnership 2 →
Partnership 3 →

Step 2: For each, ask:
Would I still want to build with this person 10 years from now?

Do our values and vision align beyond short-term wins?

Step 3: Write your "Long-Term Move" for each relationship.
Partnership 1 → (e.g., invest deeper, formalize trust, create shared commitments)

Partnership 2 → (e.g., clarify alignment, set expectations, test long-term potential)

Partnership 3 → (e.g., step back if trust is shallow or vision diverges)

Decision Filter Questions
Will this partnership still matter in 10 years?
Am I choosing alignment or just convenience?
Does this relationship multiply or drain trust over time?

This Week, I Will Invest In Long-Term People By:

PRINCIPLE #7

WEALTH WITHOUT PURPOSE IS POVERTY IN DISGUISE

The Core Idea:
Money is a multiplier. With purpose, it fuels transformation. Without it, it multiplies emptiness.

Why It Matters:
Wealth without meaning becomes a prison. Purpose turns resources into impact.

How It Helps:
By tying income to impact, I ensure fulfillment, not just financial gain.

The Outcome:
I remain fulfilled, not just paid.

Reflection

Where am I chasing money without linking it to purpose?

How would my choices change if purpose directed every financial decision?

What impact do I want my wealth to create beyond myself?

WORKBOOK EXERCISE: PURPOSE ALIGNMENT

Step 1: Identify three areas where I use or pursue money.
Business →
Personal →
Community →

Step 2: For each, ask:
What is the purpose behind this pursuit?

How can I align this use of money with impact and meaning?

Step 3: Write your "Purpose Shift" for each area.

Business → (e.g., reinvest profits into meaningful projects)

Personal → (e.g., use resources to grow, learn, and contribute)

Community → (e.g., dedicate wealth to causes that outlive me)

Decision Filter Questions

Is this about impact or just income?
Would I still pursue this if money wasn't the reward?
Does this build freedom, or just more consumption?

This Week, I Will Align My Wealth With Purpose By:

PRINCIPLE #8

STRATEGY OVER EMOTION

The Core Idea:
I act based on leverage and logic, not fear, pride, or urgency.

Why It Matters:
Emotion is fuel, but strategy is steering. If I let feelings lead, I drift off course.

How It Helps:
By acknowledging emotions but making decisions with strategy, I stay effective under pressure.

The Outcome:
I win when others panic.

Reflection

Where am I letting emotions dictate my decisions right now?

How could strategy redirect energy I usually waste on reacting?

What difference would it make if every major choice was filtered through logic first?

WORKBOOK EXERCISE: STRATEGY RESET

Step 1: List three situations where emotions often cloud my judgment.
Work →
Relationships →
Finances →

Step 2: For each, ask:
What is the emotion I usually feel here?

What strategy could I use to respond differently?

Step 3: Write your "Strategy Shift" for each area.

Work → (e.g., pause before responding, run decisions through data)

Relationships → (e.g., listen fully before reacting, focus on outcome not ego)

Finances → (e.g., avoid impulsive moves, stick to long-term plan)

Decision Filter Questions

Am I reacting from fear or deciding from clarity?

Does this action align with strategy or with emotion?

If I removed the emotion, would I still make the same choice?

This Week, I Will Choose Strategy Over Emotion By:

PRINCIPLE #9

BURN THE OLD MAPS

The Core Idea:
I don't follow paths built for someone else. I create new terrain.

Why It Matters:
Old paths lead to old destinations. If I want new outcomes, I must chart my own way.

How It Helps:
By designing from first principles instead of tradition, I escape outdated rules.

The Outcome:
I build new categories, not recycled careers.

Reflection

Where am I still following a path that doesn't fit me?

What "maps" (traditions, systems, expectations) need to be left behind?

What new ground am I being called to chart?

WORKBOOK EXERCISE: MAP BREAKER

Step 1: Identify three areas where I am following someone else's path.
Career →
Business →
Lifestyle →

Step 2: For each, ask:
What map am I following here?

What would my own map look like?

Step 3: Write your "New Map Move" for each area.

Career → (e.g., design a new role, build a unique business)

Business → (e.g., abandon outdated models, create new categories)

Lifestyle → (e.g., craft routines that fit my design, not expectations)

Decision Filter Questions

Am I building from first principles or tradition?
Does this path fit me, or was it drawn for someone else?
Will this lead me to a destination I actually want?

This Week, I Will Burn An Old Map By:

PRINCIPLE #10

BE DANGEROUS, BUT DISCIPLINED

The Core Idea:
Power must be guided. I stay sharp, but I wield it with care.

Why It Matters:
Strength without control destroys. Discipline turns raw power into precision.

How It Helps:
By training and restraining my strength, I become trusted under pressure.

The Outcome:
I remain sharp, capable, and reliable when it matters most.

Reflection
> Where in my life am I strong but undisciplined?

> How could discipline turn my raw energy into real influence?

> What would change if others knew they could always trust my control?

WORKBOOK EXERCISE: POWER AND CONTROL

Step 1: Identify three areas where I have strength or talent.
> Skill 1 →
> Skill 2 →
> Skill 3 →

Step 2: For each, ask:
> How am I currently managing this strength?

> Where is discipline missing?

Step 3: Write your "Discipline Move" for each area.

Skill 1 → (e.g., practice consistently, apply structure, set limits)

Skill 2 → (e.g., channel energy into training, refine technique)

Skill 3 → (e.g., focus on precision, avoid reckless shortcuts)

Decision Filter Questions

Am I wielding this power with discipline or recklessness?
Does this choice build trust or erode it?
Am I sharpening my strength or letting it dull?

This Week, I Will Be Dangerous But Disciplined By:

PRINCIPLE #11

BUILD FOR IMPACT, NOT JUST INCOME

The Core Idea:
If it doesn't echo after I'm gone, it wasn't big enough.

Why It Matters:
The world doesn't need more noise: it needs transformation. Income fades; impact compounds.

How It Helps:
By prioritizing depth over width, I build work that outlives the paycheck.

The Outcome:
My work becomes legacy, not just commerce.

Reflection

Where am I chasing income without impact?

What parts of my work could outlast me if built with depth?

How would my choices shift if impact was the primary metric?

WORKBOOK EXERCISE: IMPACT AUDIT

Step 1: List three areas of my work or life where I produce results.
Business →
Creative →
Community →

Step 2: For each, ask:
Does this create impact or just income?

How could I design it to echo after I'm gone?

Step 3: Write your "Impact Move" for each area.

Business → (e.g., build scalable systems that empower others)

Creative → (e.g., create work that carries meaning, not just profit)

Community → (e.g., invest time where lives are truly changed)

Decision Filter Questions

Does this create transformation or just transaction?
Would I still pursue this if it paid nothing?
Will this matter 10 years from now?

This Week, I Will Build For Impact By:

PRINCIPLE #12

NEVER OUTSOURCE THE FINAL DECISION

The Core Idea:
Advice is welcome, but the weight is mine. I decide.

Why It Matters:
I live with the outcome. If I delegate the decision, I also delegate the responsibility.

How It Helps:
I seek counsel, but I own the call. This protects accountability and clarity.

The Outcome:
I take responsibility for both wins and losses.

Reflection

Where am I letting others carry the weight of decisions I should own?

How often do I confuse collaboration with outsourcing responsibility?

What decision do I need to take full ownership of right now?

WORKBOOK EXERCISE: DECISION OWNERSHIP

Step 1: Identify three current decisions in front of me.
Decision 1 →
Decision 2 →
Decision 3 →

Step 2: For each, ask:
Who is making the final call? Me or someone else?

Am I willing to own the outcome completely?

Step 3: Write my "Ownership Move" for each decision.

    Decision 1 → (e.g., weigh counsel, then decide myself)

    Decision 2 → (e.g., stop waiting for approval, make the call)

    Decision 3 → (e.g., accept the consequence and move forward)

Decision Filter Questions

    Am I making this decision, or letting someone else do it for me?
    Will I own this outcome, good or bad?
    Am I confusing advice with authority?

This Week, I Will Own The Decision On:

PRINCIPLE #13

FIND THE SIGNAL IN SUFFERING

The Core Idea:
Pain is a teacher. I don't waste it. I transmute it.

Why It Matters:
Suffering clarifies what matters most. It sharpens values and vision.

How It Helps:
By asking better questions in hard seasons, I uncover wisdom and growth.

The Outcome:
I use hardship as raw material for resilience and alignment.

Reflection

What pain in my life have I ignored instead of learning from?

How might suffering be revealing clarity I couldn't see before?

What growth could come if I used this season as training, not punishment?

WORKBOOK EXERCISE: PAIN TO PURPOSE

Step 1: Identify three moments of recent or past suffering.
Experience 1 →
Experience 2 →
Experience 3 →

Step 2: For each, ask:
What truth or lesson did this reveal?

How could I use it to grow stronger?

Step 3: Write my "Signal Shift" for each.

Experience 1 → (e.g., built endurance, clarified values)

Experience 2 → (e.g., revealed who I can rely on)

Experience 3 → (e.g., exposed what doesn't truly matter)

Decision Filter Questions

What is this pain trying to teach me?
Am I resisting the lesson or embracing it?
Will I waste this hardship or let it shape me?

This Week, I Will Turn Suffering Into Signal By:

PRINCIPLE #14

INTEGRITY IS THE REAL INFINITE CHEAT CODE

The Core Idea:
Truth compounds. Lies subtract. I play long, and I play clean.

Why It Matters:
Integrity scales over time. Deception collapses eventually.

How It Helps:
By choosing truth consistently, I earn trust without trying.

The Outcome:
I never have to look over my shoulder.

Reflection

Where in my life am I tempted to cut corners or bend truth?

What cost have I paid in the past for ignoring integrity?

How might my influence grow if I made integrity my permanent default?

WORKBOOK EXERCISE: INTEGRITY COMPASS

Step 1: List three areas where my integrity is most tested.
Work →
Relationships →
Finances →

Step 2: For each, ask:
Where am I tempted to compromise?

What would full integrity look like here?

Step 3: Write my "Integrity Move" for each.

Work → (e.g., be transparent even when it costs me)

Relationships → (e.g., choose honesty over comfort)

Finances → (e.g., keep every commitment, even small ones)

Decision Filter Questions

Does this decision increase trust or erode it?
If this was public tomorrow, would I be proud of it?
Am I building truth that compounds, or lies that collapse?

This Week, I Will Strengthen Integrity By:

PRINCIPLE #15

BUILD WHAT OUTLASTS YOU

The Core Idea:
Not just to succeed, but to leave something that doesn't need me to keep running.

Why It Matters:
My time is finite. My impact doesn't have to be.

How It Helps:
By building legacy infrastructure, I design systems that continue beyond my presence.

The Outcome:
I create something others can inherit and expand.

Reflection

What in my life currently depends too much on me?

How could I design my work so it lasts after I'm gone?

What legacy do I want to leave that others can carry forward?

WORKBOOK EXERCISE: LEGACY BUILDER

Step 1: Identify three areas where I want impact to outlast me.
Business →
Family →
Community →

Step 2: For each, ask:
What structure or system would make this sustainable?

How can I build it to thrive without me?

Step 3: Write my "Legacy Move" for each area.

Business → (e.g., delegate leadership, create repeatable systems)

Family → (e.g., establish traditions, teach values directly)

Community → (e.g., create initiatives that stand independent of me)

Decision Filter Questions

Will this last if I step away?
Am I building dependency or durability?
Would I be proud to hand this down?

This Week, I Will Build For Legacy By:

PRINCIPLE #16

IF THE GAME IS RIGGED, CHANGE THE GAME

The Core Idea:
I don't ask to be let in. I build the door. I write the rules.

Why It Matters:
Systems weren't designed for everyone to win. If I play by broken rules, I inherit broken results.

How It Helps:
By creating new structures, I stop begging and start building.

The Outcome:
I become the gatekeeper, not the outsider.

Reflection

Where am I still asking for permission to play by someone else's rules?

What system in my life or work feels rigged against me?

How could I rewrite the rules instead of complaining about them?

WORKBOOK EXERCISE: GAME CHANGER

Step 1: Identify three areas where the current system doesn't serve me.
Business →
Finances →
Career →

Step 2: For each, ask:
What rules are keeping me stuck?

What would a better system look like if I designed it?

Step 3: Write my "New Game Move" for each area.

Business → (e.g., create my own platform instead of waiting for access)

Finances → (e.g., build my own capital structure instead of relying on lenders)

Career → (e.g., launch a new venture instead of chasing titles)

Decision Filter Questions

Am I playing a game I can actually win?
Is this system designed for my growth, or for my limits?
What would it look like to build a better game?

This Week, I Will Change The Game By:

PRINCIPLE #17

YOUR NAME IS A CONTRACT

The Core Idea:
When I put my name on something, it becomes a reflection of who I am.

Why It Matters:
Every signature, commitment, or promise either compounds respect or erodes it.

How It Helps:
By only attaching my name to what I can honor, I build credibility that multiplies.

The Outcome:
My name earns compound respect.

Reflection

Where am I attaching my name to things that don't fully reflect me?

How could I raise the standard for what deserves my signature?

If my name is a contract, what reputation am I building?

WORKBOOK EXERCISE: NAME INTEGRITY AUDIT

Step 1: Identify three commitments I currently have.
Commitment 1 →
Commitment 2 →
Commitment 3 →

Step 2: For each, ask:
Does this reflect my true standards?

Am I proud to have my name tied to this?

Step 3: Write my "Name Move" for each area.
Commitment 1 → (e.g., double down and deliver with excellence)

Commitment 2 → (e.g., exit gracefully if it no longer aligns)

Commitment 3 → (e.g., raise the quality of my involvement)

Decision Filter Questions
Would I still sign my name if this were public tomorrow?
Does this commitment honor my reputation or risk it?
Am I treating my name like a contract or a casual label?

This Week, I Will Honor My Name By:

PRINCIPLE #18

PRESSURE REVEALS, IT DOESN'T CREATE

The Core Idea:
Crisis doesn't make me: it exposes me. Pressure shows the foundation beneath.

Why It Matters:
When the storm comes, I don't rise to the occasion. I fall to my preparation.

How It Helps:
By welcoming pressure, I see what's real in me and where I need growth.

The Outcome:
I emerge forged, not fragile.

Reflection

How have past crises revealed my true preparation?

Where do I currently avoid pressure instead of letting it sharpen me?

What would I learn if I leaned into pressure instead of resisting it?

WORKBOOK EXERCISE: PRESSURE TEST

Step 1: List three areas of my life currently under pressure.
Work →
Health →
Relationships →

Step 2: For each, ask:
What is pressure revealing here?

What weaknesses or strengths is it exposing?

Step 3: Write my "Pressure Move" for each area.

Work → (e.g., address the system gaps pressure is exposing)

Health → (e.g., strengthen resilience under stress)

Relationships → (e.g., test trust and communication under strain)

Decision Filter Questions

Is this pressure exposing weakness or sharpening strength?
Am I learning from the test or just resenting it?
What foundation is this crisis revealing?

This Week, I Will Let Pressure Reveal Truth By:

PRINCIPLE #19

BUILD MOATS, NOT JUST CASTLES

The Core Idea:
A shiny win means nothing if it can't be defended.

Why It Matters:
It's not enough to succeed once. True strength is building something that endures.

How It Helps:
By designing durability into everything, I protect my work from being easily copied or destroyed.

The Outcome:
What I build can't be easily replaced.

Reflection

Where in my life or business have I built castles without moats?

What protections could I add that would defend what I've created?

How would my results change if durability was my first priority?

WORKBOOK EXERCISE: MOAT BUILDER

Step 1: Identify three areas where I've achieved a "castle" (a win, result, or success).
Area 1 →
Area 2 →
Area 3 →

Step 2: For each, ask:
How defensible is this success?

What moat would protect it from being lost or copied?

Step 3: Write my "Moat Move" for each area.

Area 1 → (e.g., protect IP, strengthen client relationships)

Area 2 → (e.g., diversify revenue streams, build stronger contracts)

Area 3 → (e.g., secure unique assets, create irreplaceable trust)

Decision Filter Questions

Does this success have a moat or just a castle?
How easy would it be for someone else to take this?
Am I building defensible strength or temporary wins?

This Week, I Will Add Moats By:

PRINCIPLE #20

REPUTATION IS INTEREST ON CHARACTER

The Core Idea:
Reputation compounds quietly as a reflection of consistent character.

Why It Matters:
Image can be manufactured, but integrity creates lasting reputation.

How It Helps:
By choosing principles over performance, I build trust that grows over time.

The Outcome:
I earn long-term influence without chasing it.

Reflection

Where am I relying on image instead of integrity?

What habits are shaping my reputation right now?

How could I let character, not performance, be my reputation engine?

WORKBOOK EXERCISE: REPUTATION BUILDER

Step 1: Identify three areas where reputation is critical.
Work →
Relationships →
Community →

Step 2: For each, ask:
What character traits am I displaying here consistently?

How is that building or eroding my reputation?

Step 3: Write my "Reputation Move" for each area.

Work → (e.g., deliver consistently, communicate honestly)

Relationships → (e.g., keep promises, show up when it matters)

Community → (e.g., contribute quietly, serve reliably)

Decision Filter Questions

Does this action align with the character I want known?
If this choice was invisible, would it still build trust?
Am I chasing image or compounding reputation?

This Week, I Will Build Reputation By:

Principle #21

Serve First. Scale Second.

The Core Idea:
Value must exist before volume. Transformation before transaction.

Why It Matters:
If I try to scale without serving, I build emptiness. Real growth is built on real value.

How It Helps:
By leading with service, I earn loyalty, trust, and lasting results.

The Outcome:
My reputation grows before my revenue does.

Reflection

Where am I focused on numbers instead of value?

Who am I serving deeply before asking for scale?

How would my results change if I prioritized transformation first?

Workbook Exercise: Service Alignment

Step 1: List three areas where I want to grow.
Business →
Relationships →
Community →

Step 2: For each, ask:
Am I serving or just trying to scale?

How could I create deeper value here?

Step 3: Write my "Serve First Move" for each area.

Business → (e.g., improve client outcomes before marketing for more)

Relationships → (e.g., give time and presence before asking for support)

Community → (e.g., contribute consistently before asking for recognition)

Decision Filter Questions

Does this create value before it creates volume?
Am I serving or just selling?
Would this still matter if it never scaled?

This Week, I Will Serve First By:

PRINCIPLE #22

SCARCITY IS A SIGNAL

The Core Idea:
If everyone is doing it, it's probably not worth doing. I go where others haven't.

Why It Matters:
The crowd is often wrong. Scarcity reveals hidden leverage.

How It Helps:
By pursuing the rare path, I find opportunities others overlook.

The Outcome:
I uncover untapped leverage and uncommon growth.

Reflection
Where am I still following the crowd?

What rare opportunities am I ignoring because they feel lonely?

How would my results change if I leaned into scarcity instead of avoiding it?

WORKBOOK EXERCISE: SCARCITY HUNT

Step 1: List three areas of life or business where I'm currently following the crowd.
Career →
Investments →
Lifestyle →

Step 2: For each, ask:
What is scarce here that I'm ignoring?

What would it look like to pursue the rare option?

Step 3: Write my "Scarcity Move" for each area.

Career → (e.g., pursue niche expertise, build in blue ocean markets)

Investments → (e.g., seek overlooked opportunities with high upside)

Lifestyle → (e.g., design habits that few choose but create edge)

Decision Filter Questions

Is this crowded or scarce?

Am I following noise or finding signal?

Does this choice lead to rare leverage or common results?

This Week, I Will Pursue Scarcity By:

PRINCIPLE #23

HIRE FOR ALIGNMENT FIRST

The Core Idea:
Skills can be taught. Values can't.

Why It Matters:
Skill without integrity is dangerous. Alignment sustains culture.

How It Helps:
By prioritizing values over resumes, I build teams that multiply trust and performance.

The Outcome:
Culture protects performance long-term.

Reflection

Where have I hired for skill instead of alignment?

What values do I need to protect in my team?

How would results change if culture was my first hiring filter?

WORKBOOK EXERCISE: ALIGNMENT HIRING

Step 1: List three qualities or values I want in every hire.
Value 1 →
Value 2 →
Value 3 →

Step 2: For each, ask:
Do I screen for this before skill?

How can I test for alignment early?

Step 3: Write my "Alignment Move" for future hiring.
Value 1 → (e.g., integrity checks in interviews)

Value 2 → (e.g., cultural fit scenarios)

Value 3 → (e.g., trial projects that reveal values)

Decision Filter Questions
Am I hiring for alignment or just skill?
Would I trust this person if no one was watching?
Will this hire strengthen or weaken culture?

This Week, I Will Protect Alignment In Hiring By:

PRINCIPLE #24

PROXIMITY IS POWER

The Core Idea:
I curate my circle. If I wouldn't trade places with someone, I don't take advice from them.

Why It Matters:
Who I'm around shapes what I believe is possible. Environment rewires belief.

How It Helps:
By choosing rooms that stretch me, I normalize excellence.

The Outcome:
I rise faster by surrounding myself with the right people.

Reflection

Who in my circle expands my thinking, and who limits it?

Where am I tolerating proximity to voices I shouldn't?

What would change if I only stayed close to people I respect deeply?

WORKBOOK EXERCISE: PROXIMITY AUDIT

Step 1: List three people I spend the most time with.
Person 1 →
Person 2 →
Person 3 →

Step 2: For each, ask:
Would I trade places with them in life or mindset?

Do they multiply or drain my growth?

Step 3: Write my "Proximity Move" for each.

      Person 1 → (e.g., lean in closer, ask better questions)

      Person 2 → (e.g., set boundaries, reduce time invested)

      Person 3 → (e.g., seek new mentors or peers that elevate me)

Decision Filter Questions

      Am I surrounded by people I'd want to become?

      Does this proximity expand me or limit me?

      Would I respect myself more or less if I mirrored them?

This Week, I Will Strengthen My Proximity By:

PRINCIPLE #25

COMPLEXITY IS A SIGN OF POOR DESIGN

The Core Idea:
Simplicity is strength. The more elegant the system, the more powerful the result.

Why It Matters:
Confusion kills momentum. Complexity hides weakness.

How It Helps:
By stripping away noise, I create clarity that accelerates execution.

The Outcome:
Execution becomes seamless.

Reflection

Where am I overcomplicating instead of simplifying?

What costs am I paying for confusion?

How would simplicity improve speed and results in my work or life?

WORKBOOK EXERCISE: SIMPLICITY BUILDER

Step 1: Identify three areas where things feel complex.
Work →
Systems →
Relationships →

Step 2: For each, ask:
What could be simplified here?

What is complexity hiding?

Step 3: Write my "Simplicity Move" for each.

Work → (e.g., cut unnecessary tasks, automate processes)

Systems → (e.g., consolidate tools, reduce steps)

Relationships → (e.g., communicate clearly, stop playing guessing games)

Decision Filter Questions

Does this add clarity or confusion?
Am I making this harder than it needs to be?
Would simplicity make this stronger?

This Week, I Will Fight Complexity By:

PRINCIPLE #26

DON'T JUST LEARN. INTEGRATE.

The Core Idea:
Knowledge is noise until it becomes embodied.

Why It Matters:
Information without application is useless. Integration creates transformation.

How It Helps:
By applying what I know immediately, I turn knowledge into leverage.

The Outcome:
I move from knowing to becoming.

Reflection

What knowledge have I collected but never applied?

How could I practice integration daily instead of chasing more input?

What difference would it make if I embodied the top 10% of what I already know?

WORKBOOK EXERCISE: INTEGRATION PRACTICE

Step 1: List three areas where I've gathered knowledge.
Business →
Health →
Personal Growth →

Step 2: For each, ask:
How much of this knowledge am I actually using?

What would integration look like right now?

Step 3: Write my "Integration Move" for each area.

Business → (e.g., apply strategies immediately instead of filing them away)

Health → (e.g., turn diet knowledge into daily action)

Personal Growth → (e.g., practice principles instead of collecting more books/podcasts)

Decision Filter Questions

Am I applying this knowledge or just storing it?
Does this stay in theory or become embodied practice?
What is one thing I can integrate today?

This Week, I Will Integrate By:

PRINCIPLE #27

LEVERAGE EVERYTHING

The Core Idea:
Capital, attention, talent, time: I look for asymmetric upside in every situation.

Why It Matters:
My energy is finite. Leverage multiplies results without multiplying effort.

How It Helps:
By stacking small inputs into outsized outcomes, I create exponential gains.

The Outcome:
I get more impact from fewer moves.

Reflection

Where am I working hard without multiplying my effort through leverage?

What resources or relationships am I underutilizing?

How would my results change if I thought in terms of leverage, not labor?

WORKBOOK EXERCISE: LEVERAGE HUNT

Step 1: Identify three resources I already have access to.
Capital →
Talent →
Time →

Step 2: For each, ask:
How can I multiply this instead of just spending it?

What would create 10x results with the same input?

Step 3: Write my "Leverage Move" for each resource.

Capital → (e.g., invest strategically instead of consuming)

Talent → (e.g., delegate tasks, empower others to multiply impact)

Time → (e.g., focus on high-return activities, eliminate low-value tasks)

Decision Filter Questions

Does this create asymmetry, or just more effort?
Am I multiplying or merely maintaining?
Is this the highest-leverage use of my time and energy?

This Week, I Will Create Leverage By:

PRINCIPLE #28

FEEDBACK IS A WEAPON

The Core Idea:
Even when it cuts, I collect it. Blind spots cost more than bruised ego.

Why It Matters:
Feedback reveals what I can't see. Without it, I grow slowly and wastefully.

How It Helps:
By welcoming feedback, I accelerate growth and sharpen leadership.

The Outcome:
I see blind spots early and improve faster.

Reflection

Where am I avoiding feedback because it stings?

Who do I trust to give me honest input?

How much faster could I grow if I embraced hard feedback?

WORKBOOK EXERCISE: FEEDBACK FINDER

Step 1: Identify three areas where feedback would sharpen me.
Work →
Relationships →
Skills →

Step 2: For each, ask:
Who can I ask for clear and honest input?

What questions would uncover blind spots?

Step 3: Write my "Feedback Move" for each area.
Work → (e.g., ask colleagues for direct critique)

Relationships → (e.g., invite input on how I show up)

Skills → (e.g., seek coaching or mentorship for improvement)

Decision Filter Questions
Am I resisting feedback or welcoming it?
What blind spot could this reveal?
Is my ego in the way of growth?

This Week, I Will Seek Feedback By:

PRINCIPLE #29

CRISIS IS A GROWTH CURVE IN DISGUISE

The Core Idea:
When everything breaks, it reveals where the real work needs to happen.

Why It Matters:
Crisis isn't just chaos. It's clarity. It shows me what's fragile and what's strong.

How It Helps:
By reframing crisis as growth, I evolve instead of collapsing.

The Outcome:
I use adversity as fuel for transformation.

Reflection

What past crisis became a growth curve for me?

How can I view current challenges as teachers instead of enemies?

Where is crisis showing me what needs to be rebuilt stronger?

WORKBOOK EXERCISE: CRISIS REFRAME

Step 1: Identify three crises I've faced or am facing.
Crisis 1 →
Crisis 2 →
Crisis 3 →

Step 2: For each, ask:
What truth did this crisis reveal?

How did it expose weakness or unlock growth?

Step 3: Write my "Growth Curve Move" for each crisis.
Crisis 1 → (e.g., rebuilt stronger systems after failure)

Crisis 2 → (e.g., developed resilience and adaptability)

Crisis 3 → (e.g., clarified priorities under pressure)

Decision Filter Questions
Am I seeing this as breakdown or breakthrough?
What is this crisis revealing that I must address?
Will I grow from this or just survive it?

This Week, I Will Grow Through Crisis By:

PRINCIPLE #30

BE THE CLIENT YOU WISH TO SERVE

The Core Idea:
I model the behavior I expect. I lead from the inside out.

Why It Matters:
I attract who I reflect. If I want excellent clients, I must live like one.

How It Helps:
By embodying the standards I expect, I magnetize the right partnerships.

The Outcome:
I draw in ideal relationships by being the example.

Reflection

Do I model the standards I expect from clients, partners, or teammates?

Where am I tolerating behaviors I wouldn't want reflected back at me?

How would my results shift if I embodied my ideal client fully?

WORKBOOK EXERCISE: CLIENT MIRROR

Step 1: Identify three qualities I want in ideal clients or partners.
Quality 1 →
Quality 2 →
Quality 3 →

Step 2: For each, ask:
Do I demonstrate this quality myself?

Where can I improve alignment?

Step 3: Write my "Client Mirror Move" for each quality.

Quality 1 → (e.g., communicate clearly and promptly)

Quality 2 → (e.g., honor agreements with precision)

Quality 3 → (e.g., invest fully in the process)

Decision Filter Questions

Am I living the same standards I expect?

Would I want to work with me if the roles were reversed?

Am I reflecting the values I want to attract?

This Week, I Will Model My Ideal Client By:

PRINCIPLE #31

MASTER THE BORING STUFF

The Core Idea:
Repetition. Discipline. Diligence. These are the quiet engines behind every great story.

Why It Matters:
Success hides in routine. The things most people avoid are where mastery is built.

How It Helps:
By embracing repetition, I build precision and resilience.

The Outcome:
Excellence becomes automatic.

Reflection

Where am I avoiding the boring work that builds mastery?

What daily discipline could change everything if I stuck with it?

How would my results shift if I embraced repetition instead of resenting it?

WORKBOOK EXERCISE: DISCIPLINE AUDIT

Step 1: List three "boring" areas I tend to avoid.
Work →
Health →
Personal →

Step 2: For each, ask:
What would consistent repetition here create?

What keeps me from embracing it?

Step 3: Write my "Discipline Move" for each.

Work → (e.g., refine small details daily, review processes)

Health → (e.g., repeat workouts, commit to meal planning)

Personal → (e.g., practice skills daily, maintain habits)

Decision Filter Questions

Am I embracing discipline or avoiding it?
Would mastery emerge if I repeated this daily?
Is boredom hiding my breakthrough?

This Week, I Will Master The Boring Stuff By:

PRINCIPLE #32

VOLUME BEFORE PRECISION

The Core Idea:
Start messy. Start loud. Perfection is a reward, not a prerequisite.

Why It Matters:
Waiting for perfect delays progress. Iteration builds mastery faster than hesitation.

How It Helps:
By shipping early, I learn faster and improve with feedback.

The Outcome:
I create momentum instead of stalling for polish.

Reflection

Where am I stuck waiting for perfection instead of producing?

How would more volume speed up my growth curve?

What could I learn faster by releasing sooner?

WORKBOOK EXERCISE: SHIP FAST

Step 1: Identify three projects or goals I've delayed for perfection.
Project 1 →
Project 2 →
Project 3 →

Step 2: For each, ask:
What would "version 1" look like if I shipped today?

What would I learn from immediate release?

Step 3: Write my "Volume Move" for each project.

Project 1 → (e.g., publish draft now, refine later)

Project 2 → (e.g., launch beta, gather feedback)

Project 3 → (e.g., test publicly, adjust after results)

Decision Filter Questions

Am I delaying progress by chasing perfect?
Would speed of learning matter more than polish here?
Is perfection protecting me from progress?

This Week, I Will Build Volume By:

PRINCIPLE #33

LEARN IN PUBLIC

The Core Idea:
I share the climb. Transparency attracts alignment and accountability.

Why It Matters:
Authenticity builds trust and invites community.

How It Helps:
By sharing openly, I attract others on the same path and accelerate growth through feedback.

The Outcome:
I grow faster with accountability and connection.

Reflection
Where am I hiding progress instead of sharing it?

How might public learning accelerate my growth?

What opportunities could emerge if I made my process visible?

WORKBOOK EXERCISE: PUBLIC LEARNING

Step 1: Identify three areas of progress I could share publicly.
Skill →
Project →
Habit →

Step 2: For each, ask:
What could I share today, even if imperfect?

How would this invite accountability or connection?

Step 3: Write my "Public Learning Move" for each.

Skill → (e.g., post progress updates, share lessons learned)

Project → (e.g., blog about the build, show behind-the-scenes)

Habit → (e.g., track consistency publicly, invite community support)

Decision Filter Questions

Am I hiding progress out of fear?
Would sharing this accelerate growth?
Does transparency build trust here?

This Week, I Will Learn In Public By:

PRINCIPLE #34

SAY LESS, MEAN MORE

The Core Idea:
Clarity is power. Brevity is strength.

Why It Matters:
Words are currency. Wasted ones dilute impact.

How It Helps:
By cutting noise and speaking with precision, my message lands harder.

The Outcome:
I communicate with authority and influence.

Reflection

Where do I use too many words instead of sharp clarity?

How would brevity strengthen my influence?

What conversations or writing could be simplified for more impact?

WORKBOOK EXERCISE: CLARITY CUT

Step 1: Identify three areas where I communicate often.
Writing →
Meetings →
Relationships →

Step 2: For each, ask:
How many words could I cut without losing meaning?

What would sharp clarity look like?

Step 3: Write my "Clarity Move" for each area.

Writing → (e.g., reduce word count by 30%)

Meetings → (e.g., shorten agenda, get to decisions faster)

Relationships → (e.g., speak truth directly, avoid filler talk)

Decision Filter Questions

Am I saying more than necessary?
Does brevity increase impact here?
Would fewer words build stronger clarity?

This Week, I Will Say Less And Mean More By:

PRINCIPLE #35

BUILD THE BRAND BEFORE YOU NEED IT

The Core Idea:
Reputation isn't a rescue rope: it's a runway.

Why It Matters:
When opportunity arrives, it's too late to start building credibility. Identity must be planted early.

How It Helps:
By investing in brand during quiet seasons, I create momentum before I need it.

The Outcome:
Opportunity finds me before I go looking.

Reflection

Where am I underinvesting in my reputation or identity?

How would future opportunities change if I built credibility now?

What small steps could I take today to strengthen brand equity?

WORKBOOK EXERCISE: BRAND BUILDER

Step 1: Identify three areas where I need stronger brand presence.
Online →
Work →
Community →

Step 2: For each, ask:
What would building early credibility look like here?

What effort now would compound later?

Step 3: Write my "Brand Move" for each area.
Online → (e.g., publish insights, share consistent message)

Work → (e.g., deliver above expectations, develop expertise)

Community → (e.g., contribute visibly, support others' growth)

Decision Filter Questions
Am I waiting for opportunity before building credibility?
Does this action strengthen my runway?
Would this brand presence attract opportunity even without effort?

This Week, I Will Build Brand By:

PRINCIPLE #36

BORROW BELIEF UNTIL YOURS IS BUILT

The Core Idea:
Confidence can be constructed. I move forward even if all I have is faith in the process.

Why It Matters:
Waiting for certainty stalls growth. Action builds conviction faster than doubt dissolves.

How It Helps:
By leaning on borrowed belief; from mentors, process, or vision, I keep moving until confidence catches up.

The Outcome:
Action becomes the foundation for unshakable belief.

Reflection

Where am I waiting for confidence before I act?

Who or what could I borrow belief from right now?

How would momentum shift if I trusted the process instead of my doubts?

WORKBOOK EXERCISE: BELIEF BUILDER

Step 1: Identify three areas where I lack confidence.
Business →
Health →
Relationships →

Step 2: For each, ask:
Who already believes in this path?

What can I borrow to keep me moving?

Step 3: Write my "Borrowed Belief Move" for each area.

    Business → (e.g., lean on mentor's track record, trust proven process)

    Health → (e.g., follow coach's plan, rely on routine until results show)

    Relationships → (e.g., trust advice from trusted friends)

Decision Filter Questions

    Am I waiting for belief, or building it through action?
    Whose belief can I borrow right now?
    Will this step build evidence for future confidence?

This Week, I Will Borrow Belief By:

PRINCIPLE #37

YOUR ENERGY INTRODUCES YOU BEFORE YOU SPEAK

The Core Idea:
Presence creates perception. My energy is a message long before my words arrive.

Why It Matters:
People feel clarity, conviction, and congruence before they hear content.

How It Helps:
By managing energy like a resource, I create trust and influence instantly.

The Outcome:
I lead with presence that commands respect.

Reflection
What energy do I bring into rooms and relationships?

How do people feel after interacting with me?

How would my outcomes change if I managed energy with intention?

WORKBOOK EXERCISE: ENERGY AUDIT

Step 1: Identify three settings where my energy matters most.
Work →
Relationships →
Public →

Step 2: For each, ask:
What energy am I bringing now?

What energy would create trust and clarity?

Step 3: Write my "Energy Shift Move" for each.

Work → (e.g., enter calm, confident, prepared)

Relationships → (e.g., show up present, not distracted)

Public → (e.g., bring conviction, project confidence)

Decision Filter Questions

Does my energy align with my intention?
Would I trust someone who showed up the way I do?
Am I leaking or multiplying energy?

This Week, I Will Elevate My Energy By:

PRINCIPLE #38

NO ONE IS COMING. BUILD IT ANYWAY.

The Core Idea:
Entitlement kills momentum. I take the next step without waiting for rescue.

Why It Matters:
Waiting wastes time. Progress only happens when I act.

How It Helps:
By creating solutions instead of expecting them, I stay in motion.

The Outcome:
I generate momentum others can join.

Reflection

Where am I still waiting for permission, help, or rescue?

What excuses am I making instead of building?

How would progress look if I stopped waiting and just acted?

WORKBOOK EXERCISE: BUILD IT ANYWAY

Step 1: Identify three areas where I'm waiting on others.
Business →
Health →
Personal →

Step 2: For each, ask:
What can I build without waiting?

What small step could I take today?

Step 3: Write my "Build Anyway Move" for each.
Business → (e.g., launch version 1 myself)

Health → (e.g., start routine without a trainer)

Personal → (e.g., begin habit without waiting for partner/friends)

Decision Filter Questions
Am I waiting for someone else to start this?
What would happen if I built it now?
Is waiting an excuse to avoid responsibility?

This Week, I Will Build Anyway By:

PRINCIPLE #39

THE BEST DEAL IS THE ONE YOU CAN WALK AWAY FROM

The Core Idea:
Freedom is the ability to say no without flinching.

Why It Matters:
Neediness kills negotiation. Leverage comes from strength, not desperation.

How It Helps:
By holding boundaries calmly, I create stronger outcomes.

The Outcome:
I win deals from a position of power.

Reflection
Where am I too dependent on a deal or opportunity?

What would change if I was willing to walk away?

How would strength shift my negotiations?

WORKBOOK EXERCISE: DEAL AUDIT

Step 1: Identify three current or upcoming deals/opportunities.
Deal 1 →
Deal 2 →
Deal 3 →

Step 2: For each, ask:
Could I walk away without panic?

What would walking away reveal about my leverage?

Step 3: Write my "Walk Away Move" for each.
Deal 1 → (e.g., clarify boundaries, set minimums)

Deal 2 → (e.g., strengthen alternative options)

Deal 3 → (e.g., prepare exit plan in advance)

Decision Filter Questions
Can I walk away from this without fear?
Am I negotiating from strength or neediness?
Does this deal preserve my freedom?

This Week, I Will Strengthen Negotiation Power By:

PRINCIPLE #40

DON'T SCALE WHAT YOU HAVEN'T PROVEN

The Core Idea:
Growth amplifies flaws. If I scale broken systems, I break everything.

Why It Matters:
Scaling too soon multiplies mistakes. Validation protects resources and reputation.

How It Helps:
By perfecting the model first, I expand only what works.

The Outcome:
I scale what's solid, not what's shaky.

Reflection

Where am I tempted to scale before proving the model?

What weaknesses would growth expose right now?

How would results shift if I validated before expanding?

WORKBOOK EXERCISE: PROOF BEFORE SCALE

Step 1: Identify three areas I'm considering scaling.
Business →
Systems →
Habits →

Step 2: For each, ask:
Has this been proven reliable?

What validation is missing?

Step 3: Write my "Proof Move" for each area.
   Business ⟶ (e.g., test on small scale first)

   Systems ⟶ (e.g., stress-test before expansion)

   Habits ⟶ (e.g., sustain consistently before adding more)

Decision Filter Questions
   Am I scaling proof or problems?
   Is this model validated or just assumed?
   Will growth multiply strength or weakness?

This Week, I Will Prove Before Scaling By:

PRINCIPLE #41

IF IT'S NOT WRITTEN, IT'S NOT REAL

The Core Idea:
Ideas live on paper. Execution lives on a plan.

Why It Matters:
Memory is fragile. Documentation endures and creates clarity.

How It Helps:
By writing things down, I move vision into action and hold myself accountable.

The Outcome:
My goals become trackable and achievable.

Reflection

What important ideas or commitments am I keeping only in my head?

Where has lack of documentation cost me clarity or progress?

How would writing more down change my outcomes?

WORKBOOK EXERCISE: WRITE IT DOWN

Step 1: Identify three areas where I rely too much on memory.
Business →
Personal →
Relationships →

Step 2: For each, ask:
What needs to be written to make this real?

How can I track and review it?

Step 3: Write my "Documentation Move" for each area.
Business → (e.g., document workflows, record commitments)

Personal → (e.g., write down goals, track progress)

Relationships → (e.g., note promises, log agreements)

Decision Filter Questions
Is this written and trackable, or just a thought?
Would clarity improve if I documented it?
Am I treating ideas as real before they are written?

This Week, I Will Make It Real By Writing Down:

PRINCIPLE #42

WHAT YOU TOLERATE, YOU TEACH

The Core Idea:
I lead by what I allow. Standards are non-negotiable.

Why It Matters:
Compromise sets culture. People learn what's acceptable from what I tolerate.

How It Helps:
By enforcing standards consistently, I protect clarity and strength.

The Outcome:
I build cultures of accountability and respect.

Reflection

Where am I tolerating behavior I shouldn't?

What silent lessons am I teaching by what I allow?

How would my environment change if I enforced my standards fully?

WORKBOOK EXERCISE: STANDARD RESET

Step 1: Identify three areas where my standards are being compromised.
Work →
Relationships →
Self →

Step 2: For each, ask:
What am I currently tolerating?

What should I teach instead?

Step 3: Write my "Standard Move" for each area.

Work → (e.g., stop accepting missed deadlines without accountability)

Relationships → (e.g., set boundaries around respect and honesty)

Self → (e.g., stop excusing procrastination or neglect)

Decision Filter Questions

What am I teaching by tolerating this?
Does this enforce my standards or erode them?
Am I leading by clarity or contradiction?

This Week, I Will Raise My Standards By:

PRINCIPLE #43

REST IS A WEAPON, NOT A WEAKNESS

The Core Idea:
Recovery is part of resilience. I protect my margins.

Why It Matters:
Burnout destroys sustainability. Rest builds strength for the long game.

How It Helps:
By recharging intentionally, I sustain energy and performance.

The Outcome:
I stay sharp and resilient over time.

Reflection
> Where am I pushing without proper recovery?

> How has neglecting rest cost me clarity or performance?

> How would my results improve if I treated rest as essential?

WORKBOOK EXERCISE: REST RESET

Step 1: Identify three areas where I need more rest.
Physical →
Mental →
Emotional →

Step 2: For each, ask:
What rest practice is missing?

How could I protect recovery here?

Step 3: Write my "Rest Move" for each area.

Physical → (e.g., consistent sleep schedule, active recovery)

Mental → (e.g., digital breaks, focus resets)

Emotional → (e.g., time alone, quality connection)

Decision Filter Questions

Am I treating rest as weakness or weapon?
Does this decision protect or deplete my energy?
Will rest increase or reduce my resilience?

This Week, I Will Recharge By:

PRINCIPLE #44

URGENCY WITHOUT DIRECTION IS CHAOS

The Core Idea:
I move with intensity, but always with aim.

Why It Matters:
Hustle without clarity creates waste and burnout.

How It Helps:
By pairing urgency with direction, I produce precision, not panic.

The Outcome:
I execute with speed and accuracy.

Reflection

Where am I moving fast without knowing where I'm going?

How has urgency without clarity cost me in the past?

What would shift if I slowed down just enough to aim first?

WORKBOOK EXERCISE: AIM BEFORE ACTION

Step 1: Identify three areas where I often move fast.
Work →
Finances →
Relationships →

Step 2: For each, ask:
Do I have direction here?

What is the actual target?

Step 3: Write my "Aim First Move" for each area.

Work → (e.g., define priorities before hustling)

Finances → (e.g., set clear savings/investment goals)

Relationships → (e.g., clarify outcomes before reacting)

Decision Filter Questions

Am I moving with clarity or just speed?
Does this urgency have direction?
Will this energy create precision or chaos?

This Week, I Will Align Urgency With Direction By:

PRINCIPLE #45

KEEP THE SWORD SHARP, EVEN IN PEACE

The Core Idea:
I prepare before the storm. The best time to train is when I don't have to.

Why It Matters:
Crisis is inevitable. Preparation during calm seasons determines outcomes during chaos.

How It Helps:
By staying sharp, I remain ready when pressure comes.

The Outcome:
I respond with confidence instead of panic.

Reflection

Where am I neglecting preparation because things feel calm?

How has lack of readiness hurt me in the past?

What would shift if I treated peace as training ground?

WORKBOOK EXERCISE: READINESS BUILDER

Step 1: Identify three areas where I need sharper preparation.
Work →
Health →
Relationships →

Step 2: For each, ask:
What training or preparation is missing here?

How can I sharpen now before crisis comes?

Step 3: Write my "Preparation Move" for each area.
Work → (e.g., strengthen systems, review emergency plans)

Health → (e.g., train consistently, build resilience habits)

Relationships → (e.g., nurture trust, establish communication patterns)

Decision Filter Questions
Am I sharp now, or coasting because it's calm?
Would I be ready if crisis hit today?
Is peace sharpening me or softening me?

This Week, I Will Sharpen In Peace By:

PRINCIPLE #46

WHAT YOU BUILD BUILDS YOU

The Core Idea:
Every project shapes my character. I choose carefully because my work sculpts me.

Why It Matters:
The things I create don't just exist outside me, they form who I become.

How It Helps:
By selecting projects aligned with my values, I ensure my growth is intentional.

The Outcome:
I evolve with every creation.

Reflection

How have past projects shaped me for better or worse?

What current work is building me into the person I want to become?

What should I stop building because it's shaping me poorly?

WORKBOOK EXERCISE: BUILDER'S AUDIT

Step 1: List three projects I'm currently building.
Project 1 →
Project 2 →
Project 3 →

Step 2: For each, ask:
How is this project shaping me?

Is this aligned with the person I want to be?

Step 3: Write my "Alignment Move" for each project.

Project 1 → (e.g., continue because it grows resilience)

Project 2 → (e.g., adjust scope to reflect my values)

Project 3 → (e.g., exit if it no longer builds me positively)

Decision Filter Questions

Is this work shaping me or shrinking me?
Am I proud of who this project is making me?
Will this build the person I want to become?

This Week, I Will Let My Work Build Me By:

PRINCIPLE #47

WORK ETHIC WINS WHEN TALENT RESTS

The Core Idea:
Talent is common. Discipline isn't. I outlast by showing up when others stop.

Why It Matters:
Skill fades without effort. Work ethic compounds long after talent stalls.

How It Helps:
By working consistently, I create momentum talent alone can't sustain.

The Outcome:
I win through perseverance, not just potential.

Reflection

Where am I relying too much on talent instead of work ethic?

How has discipline carried me further than skill before?

What would change if I treated consistency as my greatest edge?

WORKBOOK EXERCISE: WORK ETHIC BUILDER

Step 1: Identify three areas where consistency matters most.
Business →
Health →
Skills →

Step 2: For each, ask:
Am I relying on talent here, or showing up with discipline?

What small consistent actions create the edge?

Step 3: Write my "Consistency Move" for each area.
Business → (e.g., daily outreach, relentless follow-up)

Health → (e.g., train even on low-motivation days)

Skills → (e.g., practice daily, not just when inspired)

Decision Filter Questions
Am I relying on talent or consistency?
Would steady effort outlast talent here?
Am I showing up when others rest?

This Week, I Will Strengthen Work Ethic By:

PRINCIPLE #48

MASTERY IS BOUGHT IN BOREDOM

The Core Idea:
The repetitions no one sees are the ones that matter most.

Why It Matters:
Greatness is forged in monotony, not highlight reels.

How It Helps:
By training beyond boredom, I embed skill into muscle memory.

The Outcome:
Mastery becomes natural.

Reflection

Where am I avoiding repetition because it feels boring?

How could embracing monotony take me to mastery?

What skill or craft requires more unseen practice from me?

WORKBOOK EXERCISE: MASTERY REPS

Step 1: Identify three skills I want to master.
Skill 1 →
Skill 2 →
Skill 3 →

Step 2: For each, ask:
Am I willing to train past boredom?

What reps are missing from my practice?

Step 3: Write my "Mastery Move" for each skill.

Skill 1 → (e.g., daily drills even when uninspired)

Skill 2 → (e.g., practice fundamentals repeatedly)

Skill 3 → (e.g., track reps instead of results)

Decision Filter Questions

Am I willing to embrace boredom to reach mastery?
Am I chasing highlight reels or doing the hidden work?
Will my repetitions carry me past talent?

This Week, I Will Buy Mastery In Boredom By:

PRINCIPLE #49

CELEBRATE QUIET WINS

The Core Idea:
Not every win needs applause. Progress itself is the reward.

Why It Matters:
Chasing validation makes me blind to growth. Gratitude for small steps sustains me.

How It Helps:
By acknowledging quiet victories, I stay motivated and grounded.

The Outcome:
I grow without needing external approval.

Reflection

Where do I overlook progress because it isn't flashy?

How would my confidence grow if I recognized every small win?

What quiet wins could I celebrate today?

WORKBOOK EXERCISE: QUIET WINS JOURNAL

Step 1: Identify three recent small wins.
Win 1 →
Win 2 →
Win 3 →

Step 2: For each, ask:
What progress does this represent?

Why does it matter for my bigger journey?

Step 3: Write my "Celebration Move" for each.

Win 1 → (e.g., journal about the progress)

Win 2 → (e.g., acknowledge growth privately)

Win 3 → (e.g., share gratitude with someone close)

Decision Filter Questions

Am I overlooking progress because it isn't loud?
Would celebrating small wins strengthen momentum?
Am I chasing applause or acknowledging growth?

This Week, I Will Celebrate Quiet Wins By:

PRINCIPLE #50

STAY HUNGRY. STAY HUMBLE. STAY BUILDING.

The Core Idea:
The climb never ends. Success should sharpen me, not soften me.

Why It Matters:
Pride dulls the edge. Complacency kills growth.

How It Helps:
By staying a student and a builder, I ensure constant progress.

The Outcome:
I keep growing regardless of external praise.

Reflection

Where have I become complacent instead of hungry?

What would humility add to my current stage of success?

How can I keep building even after wins?

WORKBOOK EXERCISE: HUNGER CHECK

Step 1: Identify three areas where I've grown comfortable.
Area 1 →
Area 2 →
Area 3 →

Step 2: For each, ask:
How can I reignite hunger here?

What move would keep me humble and building?

Step 3: Write my "Hunger Move" for each area.

Area 1 → (e.g., set bigger goals)

Area 2 → (e.g., return to learning mindset)

Area 3 → (e.g., build something new instead of coasting)

Decision Filter Questions

Am I still hungry here?
Am I letting pride replace humility?
Am I still building or just maintaining?

This Week, I Will Stay Hungry And Humble By:

PRINCIPLE #51

NEVER LET EGO CLOSE A DOOR THAT HUMILITY COULD OPEN

The Core Idea:
Pride can cost partnerships. Humility keeps doors open.

Why It Matters:
Ego creates walls, but humility creates bridges.

How It Helps:
By choosing growth over pride, I preserve opportunities and relationships.

The Outcome:
I keep allies close and options open.

Reflection

Where has ego cost me opportunities in the past?

What relationship could humility repair or strengthen today?

How would my outcomes improve if I chose humility more often?

WORKBOOK EXERCISE: EGO CHECK

Step 1: Identify three situations where pride often shows up.
Work →
Relationships →
Negotiations →

Step 2: For each, ask:
What would humility look like here?

How could humility change the outcome?

Step 3: Write my "Humility Move" for each situation.

Work → (e.g., accept correction without defensiveness)

Relationships → (e.g., apologize first when needed)

Negotiations → (e.g., listen fully before pushing my agenda)

Decision Filter Questions

Am I protecting my pride or protecting the relationship?
Would humility open a door here?
Is ego leading me or limiting me?

This Week, I Will Choose Humility By:

PRINCIPLE #52

BUILD WEALTH THAT CAN'T BE MEASURED IN DOLLARS

The Core Idea:
Trust, loyalty, and peace of mind are the real assets.

Why It Matters:
Financial wealth without relational and spiritual wealth is shallow.

How It Helps:
By prioritizing relationships, peace, and integrity, I build wealth that outlasts money.

The Outcome:
I live rich, not just look rich.

Reflection
> Where am I defining wealth too narrowly?

> What non-financial wealth have I neglected?

> How would my life change if I treated peace and trust as assets?

WORKBOOK EXERCISE: WEALTH REDEFINED

Step 1: Identify three forms of wealth beyond money.
> Relationships →
> Health →
> Purpose →

Step 2: For each, ask:
> How am I currently investing in this?

> What would greater investment look like?

Step 3: Write my "True Wealth Move" for each area.

Relationships → (e.g., spend more intentional time)

Health → (e.g., invest in routines that preserve vitality)

Purpose → (e.g., dedicate resources to meaningful work)

Decision Filter Questions

Does this build wealth that outlasts money?

Am I richer in dollars or in trust, peace, and meaning?

Will this still matter if money disappears?

This Week, I Will Build True Wealth By:

PRINCIPLE #53

MAKE IT EASY TO SAY YES

The Core Idea:
Clarity, value, and timing beat persuasion every time.

Why It Matters:
Friction kills momentum. The easier the decision, the faster the yes.

How It Helps:
By simplifying offers and removing barriers, I create irresistible clarity.

The Outcome:
Partnerships close faster and stronger.

Reflection

Where am I overcomplicating my asks or offers?

What would happen if I made decisions effortless for others?

How could I present more clarity and value upfront?

WORKBOOK EXERCISE: YES BUILDER

Step 1: Identify three current opportunities or offers.
Opportunity 1 →
Opportunity 2 →
Opportunity 3 →

Step 2: For each, ask:
Is this simple and clear?

What friction could I remove?

Step 3: Write my "Yes Move" for each.

Opportunity 1 → (e.g., shorten pitch, show clear benefits)

Opportunity 2 → (e.g., offer simple next step)

Opportunity 3 → (e.g., reduce complexity or barriers)

Decision Filter Questions

Is this easy to say yes to?
Am I creating clarity or confusion?
Does this remove friction or add it?

This Week, I Will Make It Easy To Say Yes By:

PRINCIPLE #54

DON'T JUST SOLVE PROBLEMS. ELIMINATE THEM AT THE ROOT.

The Core Idea:
I don't put out fires. I redesign the system so fires can't start.

Why It Matters:
Band-aids create bigger messes. Root solutions prevent repeat chaos.

How It Helps:
By addressing causes instead of symptoms, I save time, energy, and trust.

The Outcome:
I create lasting stability.

Reflection

Where am I just patching problems instead of eliminating them?

What root issues have I ignored for too long?

How would things change if I solved at the source?

WORKBOOK EXERCISE: ROOT FIX

Step 1: Identify three recurring problems in my life or work.
Problem 1 →
Problem 2 →
Problem 3 →

Step 2: For each, ask:
What is the true root cause?

What system change would prevent it from recurring?

Step 3: Write my "Root Solution Move" for each problem.

Problem 1 → (e.g., create clear process instead of redoing work)

Problem 2 → (e.g., fix communication system, not just apologize)

Problem 3 → (e.g., change structure so failure can't repeat)

Decision Filter Questions

Am I solving the surface or the source?
Will this prevent the problem from coming back?
Am I redesigning or just reacting?

This Week, I Will Eliminate Problems At The Root By:

PRINCIPLE #55

POWER IS BEST USED QUIETLY

The Core Idea:
The strongest move often doesn't need an audience.

Why It Matters:
Loud leaders leak trust. Quiet strength builds influence.

How It Helps:
By letting actions speak louder than noise, I become trusted instinctively.

The Outcome:
I lead with quiet power others respect.

Reflection

Where am I trying to display power instead of using it wisely?

How could I let results, not volume, do the talking?

What would change if I practiced more quiet strength?

WORKBOOK EXERCISE: QUIET POWER PRACTICE

Step 1: Identify three areas where I use or display power.
Work →
Relationships →
Decisions →

Step 2: For each, ask:
Am I using this power loudly or quietly?

What would quiet strength look like here?

Step 3: Write my "Quiet Move" for each area.

Work → (e.g., let results speak, skip self-promotion)

Relationships → (e.g., lead with calm presence, not control)

Decisions → (e.g., act decisively without announcement)

Decision Filter Questions

Am I displaying power or applying it?
Does this move build trust or erode it?
Would quiet strength serve better here?

This Week, I Will Use Power Quietly By:

PRINCIPLE #56

PROTECT THE ASYMMETRY

The Core Idea:
I spend hours on what gives me 10x back. Most people never do.

Why It Matters:
Not all ROI is equal. High-leverage activities multiply outcomes.

How It Helps:
By protecting asymmetric opportunities, I gain disproportionate results from focused effort.

The Outcome:
I multiply outcomes while reducing wasted input.

Reflection

Where am I spending time on low-return activities?

What are the 10x activities in my life or business?

How can I protect these high-leverage moves from distraction?

WORKBOOK EXERCISE: ASYMMETRY AUDIT

Step 1: List three areas where I invest time or energy.
Business →
Health →
Personal →

Step 2: For each, ask:
What's the ROI of this activity?

Does it give me 10x back or just keep me busy?

Step 3: Write my "Asymmetry Move" for each area.
Business → (e.g., focus on strategy, delegate admin tasks)

Health → (e.g., optimize recovery for maximum output)

Personal → (e.g., prioritize key relationships over shallow ones)

Decision Filter Questions
Does this create 10x impact or 1x distraction?
Am I investing in asymmetry or wasting on symmetry?
Will this activity compound or fade?

This Week, I Will Protect The Asymmetry By:

Principle #57

Design for Scale, Operate with Intimacy

The Core Idea:
Even as I grow, I stay close to the signal.

Why It Matters:
Scale shouldn't erase soul. Growth without intimacy creates distance.

How It Helps:
By designing scalable systems while staying human, I build expansion that feels personal.

The Outcome:
Growth feels connected, not transactional.

Reflection

Where has growth created distance in my work or relationships?

How can I design systems that scale without losing soul?

What would intimacy look like at scale?

Workbook Exercise: Scale with Soul

Step 1: Identify three areas where I'm scaling.
Business →
Relationships →
Community →

Step 2: For each, ask:
How can I keep intimacy alive here?

What system could help scale without disconnecting?

Step 3: Write my "Scale Move" for each area.

Business → (e.g., personalize communication even at volume)

Relationships → (e.g., maintain rituals despite growth)

Community → (e.g., build scalable engagement systems with personal touch)

Decision Filter Questions

Am I scaling at the cost of soul?
Does this system keep me close to the signal?
Will growth feel personal or mechanical?

This Week, I Will Design For Scale With Intimacy By:

PRINCIPLE #58

STOP EXPLAINING TO PEOPLE WHO DON'T WANT TO UNDERSTAND

The Core Idea:
I protect my energy from unqualified opinions.

Why It Matters:
Misunderstood energy is wasted energy. Some people aren't ready to hear truth.

How It Helps:
By focusing on those who are willing, I maximize clarity and impact.

The Outcome:
I lead with focus, not frustration.

Reflection

Where am I wasting time trying to convince the unwilling?

Who in my life drains clarity instead of embracing it?

How would my results improve if I stopped over-explaining?

WORKBOOK EXERCISE: ENERGY PROTECTION

Step 1: Identify three situations where I over-explain.
Work →
Relationships →
Community →

Step 2: For each, ask:
Does this person want to understand?

Is my explanation productive or wasted?

Step 3: Write my "Stop Explaining Move" for each.

Work → (e.g., provide clarity once, then move on)

Relationships → (e.g., stop convincing, start modeling)

Community → (e.g., focus on those ready to engage)

Decision Filter Questions

Am I explaining to the willing or the unwilling?
Does this invest energy or drain it?
Will silence serve better than more words?

This Week, I Will Stop Over-Explaining By:

PRINCIPLE #59

MAKE YOUR ABSENCE FELT, NOT YOUR PRESENCE TOLERATED

The Core Idea:
Value is measured by impact, not noise.

Why It Matters:
Legacy is proven when things change in my absence, not just my presence.

How It Helps:
By contributing meaningful value, I ensure my presence isn't a burden but my absence is noticed.

The Outcome:
I become essential without needing the spotlight.

Reflection

Am I adding value that lasts when I'm gone, or just taking up space?

How can I shift from seeking attention to building impact?

What difference would people feel if I stepped away today?

WORKBOOK EXERCISE: ABSENCE AUDIT

Step 1: Identify three areas where my presence is most consistent.
Work →
Relationships →
Community →

Step 2: For each, ask:
Would my absence be felt here? Why or why not?

What value could I add that lasts beyond me?

Step 3: Write my "Absence Move" for each area.

Work → (e.g., create systems others depend on)

Relationships → (e.g., add depth and reliability)

Community → (e.g., contribute value that echoes)

Decision Filter Questions

Would my absence here be noticed?
Am I leaving lasting value or just filling space?
Does my presence elevate or just exist?

This Week, I Will Make My Absence Felt By:

PRINCIPLE #60

CONFIDENCE COMES FROM EVIDENCE

The Core Idea:
Belief is built by keeping promises to myself.

Why It Matters:
Confidence isn't magic, it's proof repeated until it compounds.

How It Helps:
By stacking wins and honoring commitments, I build unshakable self-trust.

The Outcome:
I walk with earned conviction.

Reflection

Where am I seeking confidence without evidence?

What promises to myself have I kept, and which have I broken?

How would my self-belief grow if I stacked small wins daily?

WORKBOOK EXERCISE: EVIDENCE BUILDER

Step 1: Identify three areas where I want more confidence.
Business →
Health →
Personal →

Step 2: For each, ask:
What small promise can I keep today?

How will I track evidence of progress?

Step 3: Write my "Evidence Move" for each area.
  Business → (e.g., complete daily outreach goal)

  Health → (e.g., keep workout schedule)

  Personal → (e.g., follow through on learning commitment)

Decision Filter Questions
  Do I have evidence for this belief?
  Am I keeping promises to myself?
  Would stacking wins increase confidence here?

This Week, I Will Build Confidence With Evidence By:

PRINCIPLE #61

SHOW UP READY, NOT NEEDY

The Core Idea:
I come with something to offer, not something to beg for.

Why It Matters:
Desperation dilutes influence.

How It Helps:
I bring solutions, not needs.

The Outcome:
I negotiate from power.

Reflection

Where am I showing up with need instead of readiness?

How do people experience my presence, as prepared or desperate?

What would change if I always led with value instead of requests?

WORKBOOK EXERCISE: READINESS CHECK

Step 1: Identify three upcoming situations where I'll engage with others.
Meeting →
Opportunity →
Relationship →

Step 2: For each, ask:
What value can I bring?

How do I prepare so I show up ready, not needy?

Step 3: Write my "Ready Move" for each situation.
Meeting → (e.g., come with researched insights)

Opportunity → (e.g., present prepared solutions)

Relationship → (e.g., bring energy, not demands)

Decision Filter Questions
Am I offering value or asking for it?
Would I respect someone who showed up like me?
Does this posture project strength or neediness?

This Week, I Will Show Up Ready By:

PRINCIPLE #62

OPERATE LIKE IT'S ALREADY YOURS

The Core Idea:
Ownership is a mindset long before it's a title.

Why It Matters:
Mindset precedes results.

How It Helps:
I carry ownership energy into every room.

The Outcome:
I'm treated like I already belong.

Reflection

Where am I waiting for permission to think and act like an owner?

How has ownership mindset shifted results for me in the past?

What spaces would treat me differently if I carried myself as if it already belonged to me?

WORKBOOK EXERCISE: OWNERSHIP MINDSET

Step 1: Identify three areas where I feel like an outsider.
Business →
Skills →
Relationships →

Step 2: For each, ask:
What would it look like to operate like I already own this?

How would ownership energy change outcomes here?

Step 3: Write my "Ownership Move" for each area.
   Business → (e.g., speak confidently, act decisively)

   Skills → (e.g., train daily like a professional, not a hobbyist)

   Relationships → (e.g., show up with responsibility, not passivity)

Decision Filter Questions
   Am I thinking like a guest or an owner?
   Would ownership energy change how I show up?
   Do I already belong here by how I carry myself?

This Week, I Will Operate Like It's Already Mine By:

PRINCIPLE #63

LET THE WORK SPEAK SO LOUD THEY FORGET TO ASK FOR CREDENTIALS

The Core Idea:
I don't explain. I deliver.

Why It Matters:
Results silence doubt.

How It Helps:
I overdeliver instead of overselling.

The Outcome:
My work earns more respect than my title.

Reflection
Where am I over-explaining instead of letting results speak?

How could I let execution be my loudest message?

What projects or outcomes already prove my credibility?

WORKBOOK EXERCISE: WORK SPEAKS

Step 1: Identify three areas where results matter more than words.
Business →
Personal Growth →
Relationships →

Step 2: For each, ask:
Am I over-talking or over-delivering?

What would silence the doubt with proof?

Step 3: Write my "Proof Move" for each area.
Business → (e.g., deliver excellence, not hype)

Personal Growth → (e.g., demonstrate consistency, not promises)

Relationships → (e.g., show loyalty in action, not declarations)

Decision Filter Questions

Does my work speak louder than my words?
Would results here silence the need for credentials?
Am I overselling or overdelivering?

This Week, I Will Let The Work Speak By:

Principle #64

Learn Fast. Adjust Faster.

The Core Idea:
Speed of adaptation is survival. I don't fear being wrong, I fear being stuck.

Why It Matters:
Slow learners get left behind.

How It Helps:
I update my beliefs and models in real time.

The Outcome:
I stay relevant and resilient.

Reflection

Where am I holding onto outdated models?

How quickly do I adapt when conditions change?

What belief or system needs an update right now?

Workbook Exercise: Adaptation Sprint

Step 1: Identify three areas where I've recently learned something new.
Business →
Health →
Relationships →

Step 2: For each, ask:
Did I integrate the lesson immediately?

What adjustment is still missing?

Step 3: Write my "Fast Adjustment Move" for each area.
Business → (e.g., pivot strategy quickly when data shifts)

Health → (e.g., change habits as feedback shows)

Relationships → (e.g., update communication when something fails)

Decision Filter Questions
Am I adapting or resisting?
Is being wrong slowing me down, or speeding me up?
Did I learn this lesson fast enough to matter?

This Week, I Will Learn And Adjust Faster By:

PRINCIPLE #65

BUILD ON FIRST PRINCIPLES, NOT TRENDS

The Core Idea:
Trends fade. Truth compounds. I build from the bedrock.

Why It Matters:
Noise fades. Fundamentals last.

How It Helps:
I anchor in timeless logic.

The Outcome:
I build things that endure.

Reflection

Where am I chasing trends instead of principles?

What timeless truths can guide my current decisions?

How would my work change if I anchored only in fundamentals?

WORKBOOK EXERCISE: FIRST PRINCIPLE BUILDER

Step 1: Identify three areas where I may be following trends.
Business →
Habits →
Investments →

Step 2: For each, ask:
What is the core principle underneath?

How can I rebuild from that foundation?

Step 3: Write my "Principle Move" for each area.

Business → (e.g., design around customer value, not hype)

Habits → (e.g., anchor on consistency, not fads)

Investments → (e.g., bet on fundamentals, not speculation)

Decision Filter Questions

Is this a principle or a passing trend?
Will this choice last beyond the moment?
Am I building on bedrock or sand?

This Week, I Will Build From First Principles By:

PRINCIPLE #66

FIGHT FOR SIMPLICITY

The Core Idea:
The more powerful the idea, the simpler its delivery. Complexity hides weakness.

Why It Matters:
Complexity is a mask.

How It Helps:
I keep things clean, lean, and actionable.

The Outcome:
Execution accelerates.

Reflection

Where am I hiding behind complexity instead of clarity?

What message or system could be cut in half and strengthened?

How has simplicity served me better than complexity in the past?

WORKBOOK EXERCISE: SIMPLICITY BUILDER

Step 1: Identify three areas where complexity slows me down.
Communication →
Business Systems →
Daily Habits →

Step 2: For each, ask:
What is unnecessary here?

How can I make this simpler without losing power?

Step 3: Write my "Simplicity Move" for each area.

Communication → (e.g., cut jargon, speak directly)

Business Systems → (e.g., remove redundant steps)

Daily Habits → (e.g., focus on essentials, not gimmicks)

Decision Filter Questions

Does this add clarity or clutter?
Would this work if explained in one sentence?
Am I building strength or hiding behind complexity?

This Week, I Will Fight For Simplicity By:

PRINCIPLE #67

PRACTICE LOUD, SO YOU CAN PERFORM QUIET

The Core Idea:
I train in public. I deliver in silence. Mastery makes the loud things effortless.

Why It Matters:
Training prepares the subconscious.

How It Helps:
I work publicly and unglamorously.

The Outcome:
I perform naturally under pressure.

Reflection

Where am I avoiding practice because it feels messy?

How would public practice accelerate my mastery?

What areas need louder training so I can perform quietly later?

WORKBOOK EXERCISE: LOUD PRACTICE

Step 1: Identify three skills or areas I need to master.
Skill 1 →
Skill 2 →
Skill 3 →

Step 2: For each, ask:
How can I practice this loudly, even if it looks messy?

What repetition will make this automatic under pressure?

Step 3: Write my "Practice Move" for each skill.
Skill 1 → (e.g., rehearse publicly, seek critique)

Skill 2 → (e.g., publish drafts, test in real environments)

Skill 3 → (e.g., role-play or simulate under observation)

Decision Filter Questions
Am I practicing enough to perform naturally?
Would louder practice remove fear of public pressure?
Is my training preparing me for silence under stress?

This Week, I Will Practice Loudly By:

PRINCIPLE #68

SEEK FRICTION THAT SHARPENS, NOT DRAINS

The Core Idea:
I welcome challenge from those who want me better, not bitter.

Why It Matters:
Conflict can create clarity.

How It Helps:
I invite feedback from people who want me to win.

The Outcome:
I refine without resentment.

Reflection

Who in my life sharpens me with truth instead of draining me with criticism?

Where am I avoiding healthy friction because it feels uncomfortable?

How could I grow faster if I embraced sharpening conflict?

WORKBOOK EXERCISE: FRICTION AUDIT

Step 1: Identify three relationships or settings where friction occurs.
Work →
Relationships →
Personal Growth →

Step 2: For each, ask:
Is this sharpening or draining me?

How can I lean into sharpening friction more?

Step 3: Write my "Sharpening Move" for each.

Work → (e.g., seek tough feedback from mentors)

Relationships → (e.g., invite truth-telling conversations)

Personal Growth → (e.g., engage in environments that challenge me)

Decision Filter Questions

Is this friction making me sharper or smaller?
Does this person want me to win or to fail?
Am I avoiding discomfort that could refine me?

This Week, I Will Seek Sharpening Friction By:

PRINCIPLE #69

DON'T AIM TO BE LIKED. AIM TO BE RESPECTED.

The Core Idea:
If I must choose, I choose truth over approval.

Why It Matters:
Approval fades. Respect sticks.

How It Helps:
I lead from conviction, not consensus.

The Outcome:
I attract what I stand for.

Reflection

Where am I chasing approval instead of respect?

What truth am I avoiding because I fear being disliked?

How would my leadership change if respect was the goal?

WORKBOOK EXERCISE: RESPECT OVER APPROVAL

Step 1: Identify three areas where I crave approval.
Work →
Social Circles →
Relationships →

Step 2: For each, ask:
Am I being liked or being respected here?

What truth would shift me from approval to respect?

Step 3: Write my "Respect Move" for each area.
Work → (e.g., speak honestly in meetings)

Social Circles → (e.g., stop softening convictions to fit in)

Relationships → (e.g., tell the truth even if it risks comfort)

Decision Filter Questions
Am I seeking to be liked or respected?
Does this choice build approval or conviction?
Would they still respect me if I said no?

This Week, I Will Pursue Respect By:

PRINCIPLE #70

BE THE ONE WHO CALLS IT FIRST

The Core Idea:
The visionary always sounds crazy, until they're proven right.

Why It Matters:
Visionaries lead the wave.

How It Helps:
I speak my insight before it's safe.

The Outcome:
I create trend, not follow it.

Reflection

Where am I waiting too long to voice what I see?

What vision am I holding back because I fear being wrong?

How would my influence grow if I spoke first with conviction?

WORKBOOK EXERCISE: VISION CALLER

Step 1: Identify three insights, trends, or opportunities I see early.
Insight 1 →
Insight 2 →
Insight 3 →

Step 2: For each, ask:
Why am I hesitating to call this out?

What would it take to voice it now?

Step 3: Write my "Call It Move" for each insight.
    Insight 1 → (e.g., publish the prediction early)

    Insight 2 → (e.g., pitch the idea before it's popular)

    Insight 3 → (e.g., commit resources while others hesitate)

Decision Filter Questions
    Am I waiting for consensus before speaking?
    Does silence cost me vision leadership?
    Would calling this first create positioning?

This Week, I Will Call It First By:

PRINCIPLE #71

GROW THE ROOTS BEFORE YOU SHOW THE LEAVES

The Core Idea:
I build depth before show. Quiet foundation, loud results.

Why It Matters:
Foundation beats flash.

How It Helps:
I build depth before display.

The Outcome:
I scale with stability.

Reflection

Where am I showing off leaves before I've grown roots?

What areas of my life need deeper foundation before visibility?

How has strong groundwork served me better than early flash in the past?

WORKBOOK EXERCISE: ROOT BUILDER

Step 1: Identify three areas where I'm tempted to show results too early.
Business →
Skills →
Relationships →

Step 2: For each, ask:
What roots must I grow here first?

How do I strengthen foundation before showing results?

Step 3: Write my "Root Move" for each area.

Business → (e.g., build systems before scaling marketing)

Skills → (e.g., train fundamentals before public performance)

Relationships → (e.g., grow trust before expecting loyalty)

Decision Filter Questions

Am I focused on roots or leaves?

Does this show flash or foundation?

Will this endure when tested?

This Week, I Will Grow Roots By:

PRINCIPLE #72

KNOW THE DIFFERENCE BETWEEN URGENT AND IMPORTANT

The Core Idea:
I prioritize what compounds, not just what screams.

Why It Matters:
Urgency steals attention.

How It Helps:
I filter noise from signal.

The Outcome:
I get the right things done.

Reflection

Where am I chasing urgency instead of importance?

What truly compounding tasks am I neglecting?

How could I better separate urgent noise from important signal?

WORKBOOK EXERCISE: URGENT VS. IMPORTANT

Step 1: Identify three tasks or responsibilities on my plate.
Task 1 →
Task 2 →
Task 3 →

Step 2: For each, ask:
Is this urgent or important?

Does this task compound over time?

Step 3: Write my "Priority Move" for each task.

Task 1 → (e.g., delegate urgency, focus on impact)

Task 2 → (e.g., protect deep work for compounding goals)

Task 3 → (e.g., eliminate busywork disguised as urgency)

Decision Filter Questions

Is this urgent or truly important?

Will this matter a year from now?

Does this task compound or just scream?

This Week, I Will Prioritize Importance By:

PRINCIPLE #73

STUDY OUTCOMES, NOT OPINIONS

The Core Idea:
I look at results, not noise, narratives, or feelings.

Why It Matters:
Most opinions aren't paid for.

How It Helps:
I look at results, not rhetoric.

The Outcome:
I copy what works, not what's loud.

Reflection

Where am I listening to opinions instead of results?

Who has outcomes I'd actually trade for?

How much energy am I wasting on rhetoric instead of evidence?

WORKBOOK EXERCISE: RESULTS FILTER

Step 1: Identify three sources of advice or input I consume.
Source 1 →
Source 2 →
Source 3 →

Step 2: For each, ask:
Do they have real outcomes?

Are their results worth replicating?

Step 3: Write my "Outcome Move" for each source.
    Source 1 → (e.g., keep if results align)

    Source 2 → (e.g., cut if it's only rhetoric)

    Source 3 → (e.g., model proven outcomes)

Decision Filter Questions
    Am I studying outcomes or opinions?
    Would I trade lives with this person giving advice?
    Is this evidence or just noise?

This Week, I Will Focus On Outcomes By:

PRINCIPLE #74

USE MONEY TO BUY TIME, NOT JUST THINGS

The Core Idea:
The highest ROI is time reclaimed for what matters.

Why It Matters:
Time is the rarest asset.

How It Helps:
I invest in leverage and peace.

The Outcome:
I live on my own schedule.

Reflection

Where am I spending money on things instead of time?

What would it look like to buy back hours instead of stuff?

How has money already freed me when used wisely?

WORKBOOK EXERCISE: TIME ROI

Step 1: Identify three areas where I spend money regularly.
Work →
Lifestyle →
Personal Growth →

Step 2: For each, ask:
Does this purchase save me time or steal it?

How could I redirect money toward freedom?

Step 3: Write my "Time Move" for each area.
Work → (e.g., delegate tasks, hire help)

Lifestyle → (e.g., pay for convenience that frees hours)

Personal Growth → (e.g., buy coaching or training to accelerate learning)

Decision Filter Questions

Does this buy freedom or just consumption?
Would I trade this money for more time?
Am I investing in things or in schedule control?

This Week, I Will Buy Time By:

PRINCIPLE #75

STOP PLAYING DEFENSE WITH YOUR LIFE

The Core Idea:
I don't just react. I impose direction.

Why It Matters:
Reaction limits potential.

How It Helps:
I design a proactive strategy.

The Outcome:
I own my outcomes.

Reflection

Where am I only reacting instead of leading?

What area of my life feels stuck on defense?

How would proactive strategy change my outcomes?

WORKBOOK EXERCISE: OFFENSE AUDIT

Step 1: Identify three areas where I play defense.
Business →
Health →
Relationships →

Step 2: For each, ask:
What would offense look like here?

How can I impose direction instead of waiting?

Step 3: Write my "Offense Move" for each area.

Business → (e.g., design strategy, not just react to markets)

Health → (e.g., create proactive training plan)

Relationships → (e.g., initiate connection, not wait for others)

Decision Filter Questions

Am I reacting or directing?
Does this choice put me on offense or defense?
Am I shaping outcomes or being shaped by them?

This Week, I Will Go On Offense By:

PRINCIPLE #76

DON'T WATER WHAT WON'T GROW

The Core Idea:
Some ideas, people, and seasons are meant to be outgrown.

Why It Matters:
Energy is finite.

How It Helps:
I let go of deadweight.

The Outcome:
I cultivate what actually multiplies.

Reflection

Where am I still investing in something that won't grow?

Who or what am I keeping alive out of comfort instead of potential?

How would my results change if I stopped watering the dead things?

WORKBOOK EXERCISE: GROWTH AUDIT

Step 1: Identify three areas where I'm investing energy.
Business →
Relationships →
Personal Projects →

Step 2: For each, ask:
Is this truly growing or just draining me?

What evidence of growth do I see?

Step 3: Write my "Growth Move" for each area.
Business → (e.g., double down on scalable projects, cut stale ones)

Relationships → (e.g., invest in reciprocal connections)

Personal Projects → (e.g., exit outdated ventures, focus on current mission)

Decision Filter Questions
Is this multiplying or stagnating?
Am I nurturing growth or clinging to comfort?
Would letting go free more energy for fertile ground?

This Week, I Will Stop Watering What Won't Grow By:

PRINCIPLE #77

BECOME IMPOSSIBLE TO REPLACE

The Core Idea:
I aim to be the person the mission can't afford to lose.

Why It Matters:
Irreplaceability is job security.

How It Helps:
I do what only I can do, better than anyone else.

The Outcome:
I build unshakable leverage.

Reflection

Where am I too replaceable in what I do?

What unique skills or strengths can I sharpen to stand apart?

How would my leverage grow if I became essential?

WORKBOOK EXERCISE: IRREPLACEABILITY MAP

Step 1: Identify three areas where I bring value.
Work →
Relationships →
Community →

Step 2: For each, ask:
Could someone easily replace me here?

What unique value can I add?

Step 3: Write my "Irreplaceable Move" for each area.
Work → (e.g., specialize in rare skill, innovate in my role)

Relationships → (e.g., become the most reliable person in their life)

Community → (e.g., contribute in ways only I can)

Decision Filter Questions
Could anyone do this role as well as me?
Am I developing unique value or common effort?
Does this make me essential or optional?

This Week, I Will Strengthen My Irreplaceability By:

PRINCIPLE #78

BUILD TRUST BEFORE YOU ASK FOR IT

The Core Idea:
Every action is a deposit. Trust is earned through consistency.

Why It Matters:
Trust is earned, not assumed.

How It Helps:
I show up consistently before I ask for commitment.

The Outcome:
People say yes because they believe me.

Reflection

Where have I expected trust without earning it?

What daily actions could rebuild or reinforce trust?

How have consistent deposits built my credibility in the past?

WORKBOOK EXERCISE: TRUST LEDGER

Step 1: Identify three relationships where trust matters most.
Relationship 1 →
Relationship 2 →
Relationship 3 →

Step 2: For each, ask:
What deposits am I making here?

Where have I withdrawn without replacing?

Step 3: Write my "Trust Move" for each.
    Relationship 1 → (e.g., show consistency in small actions)

    Relationship 2 → (e.g., follow through on promises)

    Relationship 3 → (e.g., practice transparency and honesty)

Decision Filter Questions
    Am I asking for trust I haven't earned?
    Does this action deposit or withdraw trust?
    Would I trust me if the roles were reversed?

This Week, I Will Build Trust By:

PRINCIPLE #79

CRAFT OFFERS THAT SELL THEMSELVES

The Core Idea:
I design value so clear it doesn't need convincing.

Why It Matters:
Obvious value doesn't need pressure.

How It Helps:
I stack proof, clarity, and urgency.

The Outcome:
Conversions happen naturally.

Reflection

Where am I relying on persuasion instead of proof?

How could I make my value so clear it's undeniable?

What offers in my past have sold themselves?

WORKBOOK EXERCISE: OFFER DESIGN

Step 1: Identify three offers I currently have or want to build.
Offer 1 →
Offer 2 →
Offer 3 →

Step 2: For each, ask:
Is the value obvious in seconds?

Would I buy this myself without a sales pitch?

Step 3: Write my "Offer Move" for each.

Offer 1 → (e.g., simplify explanation to one line)

Offer 2 → (e.g., add undeniable proof of results)

Offer 3 → (e.g., create urgency without pressure)

Decision Filter Questions

Would I buy this without a pitch?
Is the value so obvious it sells itself?
Does this feel like persuasion or proof?

This Week, I Will Strengthen My Offers By:

PRINCIPLE #80

LET THE RIGHT THINGS TAKE TIME

The Core Idea:
Not everything is meant to scale fast. Some things are worth building slowly.

Why It Matters:
Good things grow slow.

How It Helps:
I stay patient where it matters.

The Outcome:
I build things that last.

Reflection

Where am I rushing something that deserves patience?

What areas of my life need slower, deeper growth?

How has patience paid off for me in the past?

WORKBOOK EXERCISE: PATIENCE PRACTICE

Step 1: Identify three areas where I'm tempted to rush.
Business →
Relationships →
Personal Growth →

Step 2: For each, ask:
What would patience look like here?

How does slowing down create strength?

Step 3: Write my "Patience Move" for each area.
Business → (e.g., refine process before scaling)

Relationships → (e.g., invest in trust-building over time)

Personal Growth → (e.g., commit to long-term habits, not shortcuts)

Decision Filter Questions
Am I rushing or respecting the process?
Will this compound more if I let it take time?
Is speed serving me or sabotaging me?

This Week, I Will Let The Right Things Take Time By:

PRINCIPLE #81

AUDIT FOR ALIGNMENT OFTEN

The Core Idea:
I don't just ask "is it working?," I ask "is it still right?"

Why It Matters:
Misalignment compounds.

How It Helps:
I check goals, people, and systems regularly.

The Outcome:
I don't drift. I adjust.

Reflection

Where am I currently out of alignment?

What habits, people, or systems no longer match my direction?

How often am I checking if my path is still true?

WORKBOOK EXERCISE: ALIGNMENT AUDIT

Step 1: Identify three areas to check for alignment.
Goals →
People →
Systems →

Step 2: For each, ask:
Is this still aligned with who I am becoming?

If not, what must shift?

Step 3: Write my "Alignment Move" for each area.
Goals → (e.g., refine to match new priorities)

People → (e.g., deepen aligned relationships, exit misaligned ones)

Systems → (e.g., upgrade processes for current season)

Decision Filter Questions
Is this still aligned?
Am I drifting or directing?
Would future me thank me for staying on this track?

This Week, I Will Audit For Alignment By:

PRINCIPLE #82

LEARN TO LEAVE BEFORE YOU BREAK

The Core Idea:
Not all exits are failures. Some are wisdom.

Why It Matters:
Wisdom exits early.

How It Helps:
I leave at peak, not collapse.

The Outcome:
I pivot with grace, not regret.

Reflection

Where am I holding on too long?

What situation would be better ended early than late?

How has staying too long cost me before?

WORKBOOK EXERCISE: EXIT STRATEGY

Step 1: Identify three areas where I may be overstaying.
Work →
Relationships →
Projects →

Step 2: For each, ask:
Is this growing me or breaking me?

Would leaving now save me later?

Step 3: Write my "Exit Move" for each area.

Work → (e.g., move before burnout hits)

Relationships → (e.g., part ways with respect, not resentment)

Projects → (e.g., stop pouring into things already finished)

Decision Filter Questions

Am I staying out of fear or wisdom?
Would leaving now protect me later?
Is this exit a loss or a lesson?

This Week, I Will Leave Before Breaking By:

PRINCIPLE #83

BUILD CULTURE BEFORE YOU BUILD COMPANY

The Core Idea:
A toxic team ruins the best ideas. I build from character.

Why It Matters:
Culture scales or sinks everything.

How It Helps:
I embed values before systems.

The Outcome:
I grow with soul, not just structure.

Reflection

What culture am I building right now?

How would my team describe our values?

Where am I tolerating culture leaks that will compound?

WORKBOOK EXERCISE: CULTURE CHECK

Step 1: Identify three cultural values I want to build.
Value 1 →
Value 2 →
Value 3 →

Step 2: For each, ask:
Am I modeling this daily?

How does this shape the company environment?

Step 3: Write my "Culture Move" for each value.
Value 1 → (e.g., honesty in every meeting)

Value 2 → (e.g., celebrate wins, not egos)

Value 3 → (e.g., prioritize trust before titles)

Decision Filter Questions

Does this action strengthen or weaken culture?
Would I want to work in this environment?
Does culture lead before structure here?

This Week, I Will Build Culture By:

PRINCIPLE #84

DON'T CONFUSE VISIBILITY WITH VALUE

The Core Idea:
Not all that's seen is significant. Not all that matters is on stage.

Why It Matters:
Loud doesn't equal impactful.

How It Helps:
I focus on transformation, not trend.

The Outcome:
I become known for what actually works.

Reflection

Where am I chasing visibility instead of creating value?

What impact am I making behind the scenes that truly matters?

How can I separate applause from substance?

WORKBOOK EXERCISE: VALUE OVER VISIBILITY

Step 1: Identify three areas where I seek visibility.
Social Media →
Business →
Relationships →

Step 2: For each, ask:
Is this true value or just exposure?

How can I shift toward lasting impact?

Step 3: Write my "Value Move" for each area.

Social Media → (e.g., post insights that help, not just attract)

Business → (e.g., focus on client outcomes, not vanity metrics)

Relationships → (e.g., build private trust over public optics)

Decision Filter Questions

Does this create substance or just exposure?

Would I still do this if no one saw it?

Does this add noise or value?

This Week, I Will Focus On Value By:

PRINCIPLE #85

BUY BACK YOUR ENERGY

The Core Idea:
I delegate, automate, and eliminate so I can do what only I can do.

Why It Matters:
Energy is the limit.

How It Helps:
I cut what drains and double down on what drives.

The Outcome:
I stay energized and effective.

Reflection

Where am I wasting energy on tasks that don't matter?

What drains me more than it develops me?

How could I buy back my focus this week?

WORKBOOK EXERCISE: ENERGY AUDIT

Step 1: Identify three areas that drain my energy.
Task 1 →
Task 2 →
Task 3 →

Step 2: For each, ask:
Can I delegate, automate, or eliminate this?

What would buying back my energy look like here?

Step 3: Write my "Energy Move" for each task.

Task 1 → (e.g., outsource busywork)

Task 2 → (e.g., automate recurring processes)

Task 3 → (e.g., eliminate low-value commitments)

Decision Filter Questions

Does this give energy or drain it?
Can someone or something else do this?
Am I spending my best energy on my best work?

This Week, I Will Buy Back Energy By:

PRINCIPLE #86

MAKE YOUR MISSION BIGGER THAN YOUR MOOD

The Core Idea:
Discipline moves even when motivation doesn't.

Why It Matters:
Emotion is volatile.

How It Helps:
I commit to purpose, not convenience.

The Outcome:
I remain consistent, even on hard days.

Reflection

Where have I let moods dictate momentum?

How would my consistency change if mission led instead of feelings?

What mission is worth moving for even when I don't feel like it?

WORKBOOK EXERCISE: MISSION ANCHOR

Step 1: Identify three areas where mood often derails me.
Work →
Health →
Relationships →

Step 2: For each, ask:
What mission makes this worth pushing through?

How do I anchor discipline here?

Step 3: Write my "Mission Move" for each area.
Work → (e.g., create deadlines tied to purpose)

Health → (e.g., train for long-term vitality, not short-term mood)

Relationships → (e.g., commit to consistency in love, not convenience)

Decision Filter Questions
Am I being led by mission or by mood?
Would discipline move me forward here?
Does this serve a bigger purpose than my feelings?

This Week, I Will Put Mission Over Mood By:

PRINCIPLE #87

BECOME KNOWN FOR SOMETHING CLEAR

The Core Idea:
I narrow until I'm undeniable.

Why It Matters:
Confused brands get ignored.

How It Helps:
I specialize, then dominate.

The Outcome:
I become the obvious choice.

Reflection

What am I currently known for?

Is it clear, or is it diluted?

What would I need to specialize in to become undeniable?

WORKBOOK EXERCISE: CLARITY AUDIT

Step 1: Identify three areas of strength or skill.
Strength 1 →
Strength 2 →
Strength 3 →

Step 2: For each, ask:
Is this what I want to be known for?

Is it clear to others?

Step 3: Write my "Clarity Move" for each area.
Strength 1 → (e.g., position it visibly)

Strength 2 → (e.g., eliminate distractions)

Strength 3 → (e.g., sharpen brand message)

Decision Filter Questions
Would people describe me clearly?
Is my brand confusing or undeniable?
Am I narrowing or diluting?

This week, I will sharpen my clarity by:

CREATE OUTCOMES, NOT ACTIVITY

The Core Idea:
I measure by impact, not busyness.

Why It Matters:
Motion isn't progress.

How It Helps:
I track impact, not busyness.

The Outcome:
I move the needle.

Reflection

Where am I mistaking activity for progress?

What outcomes would actually move the needle?

How would my schedule change if I measured results only?

WORKBOOK EXERCISE: OUTCOME TRACKER

Step 1: Identify three areas where I'm busy but not effective.
Work →
Health →
Relationships →

Step 2: For each, ask:
What's the real outcome I want?

What activity doesn't serve that outcome?

Step 3: Write my "Outcome Move" for each area.

Work → (e.g., track revenue, not emails sent)

Health → (e.g., measure strength gained, not hours in gym)

Relationships → (e.g., count depth of connection, not time spent)

Decision Filter Questions

Is this outcome or activity?
Does this move the needle?
Would results prove this effort matters?

This Week, I Will Focus On Outcomes By:

PRINCIPLE #89

EXIT LOOPS THAT NO LONGER SERVE YOU

The Core Idea:
Even good habits can become cages. I evolve intentionally.

Why It Matters:
Familiarity isn't freedom.

How It Helps:
I cut cycles that cost peace.

The Outcome:
I evolve without apology.

Reflection

What loops or habits no longer serve me?

Am I repeating something just because it's familiar?

What would evolution look like here?

WORKBOOK EXERCISE: LOOP AUDIT

Step 1: Identify three recurring loops in my life.
Loop 1 →
Loop 2 →
Loop 3 →

Step 2: For each, ask:
Is this serving me or trapping me?

What would it take to exit?

Step 3: Write my "Exit Move" for each loop.

Loop 1 → (e.g., replace outdated habit with growth one)

Loop 2 → (e.g., stop repeating unproductive cycle)

Loop 3 → (e.g., leave relationships that recycle dysfunction)

Decision Filter Questions

Does this loop still serve me?
Am I staying out of habit or growth?
What would breaking it unlock?

This Week, I Will Exit Loops By:

Principle #90

Leave Everything Better Than You Found It

The Core Idea:
Whether a meeting, a partnership, or a stranger, I leave a mark.

Why It Matters:
Contribution creates legacy.

How It Helps:
I lead with value, not ego.

The Outcome:
I earn goodwill everywhere I go.

Reflection
Do I leave places better or drained?

What would happen if my focus was always contribution first?

How could I elevate people or projects daily?

Workbook Exercise: Better Builder

Step 1: Identify three environments I regularly touch.
Work →
Relationships →
Community →

Step 2: For each, ask:
Do I leave this better or worse?

What small move could improve it?

Step 3: Write my "Better Move" for each environment.

Work → (e.g., contribute solutions, not just criticism)

Relationships → (e.g., leave people encouraged, not drained)

Community → (e.g., create value in every interaction)

Decision Filter Questions

Am I leaving this better than I found it?
Would people want me back because of the value I add?
Does my presence elevate or extract?

This Week, I Will Leave Things Better By:

PRINCIPLE #91

OBSESS OVER THE DETAILS THAT MATTER

The Core Idea:
I don't sweat everything, just the right things.

Why It Matters:
Excellence hides in nuance.

How It Helps:
I sweat the right stuff.

The Outcome:
I build beauty and trust.

Reflection

Where am I sweating the wrong details?

What details, if sharpened, would elevate excellence?

How do the right details separate me from average?

WORKBOOK EXERCISE: DETAIL AUDIT

Step 1: Identify three areas where details matter most.
Work →
Health →
Relationships →

Step 2: For each, ask:
Which details create trust here?

Which details are noise?

Step 3: Write my "Detail Move" for each area.

Work → (e.g., polish presentation quality)

Health → (e.g., refine sleep schedule)

Relationships → (e.g., remember important dates, preferences)

Decision Filter Questions

Am I sweating the right details?
Does this detail build excellence or distraction?
Would this small improvement multiply trust?

This Week, I Will Sharpen Details By:

PRINCIPLE #92

PROTECT THE DOWNSIDE. THEN SWING BIG.

The Core Idea:
I de-risk ruthlessly so I can go all in when it counts.

Why It Matters:
Risk without protection is roulette.

How It Helps:
I hedge intelligently, then go all in.

The Outcome:
I take bold shots without reckless risk.

Reflection

Where am I gambling instead of managing risk?

What protections do I need before going all in?

How would downside protection free me to swing bigger?

WORKBOOK EXERCISE: RISK MAP

Step 1: Identify three major risks in front of me.
Risk 1 →
Risk 2 →
Risk 3 →

Step 2: For each, ask:
How can I protect the downside?

Once protected, where can I go bigger?

Step 3: Write my "Swing Move" for each risk.

Risk 1 → (e.g., secure backup plan, then commit)

Risk 2 → (e.g., insure or hedge against failure)

Risk 3 → (e.g., mitigate loss, then scale)

Decision Filter Questions

Have I protected the downside?
Am I swinging big enough once I'm safe?
Is this bold or reckless?

This Week, I Will Protect And Swing By:

PRINCIPLE #93

LET DATA INFORM YOU, BUT DON'T LET IT DEFINE YOU

The Core Idea:
I trust the numbers, but I move with instinct too.

Why It Matters:
Intuition plus insight wins.

How It Helps:
I balance gut and graph.

The Outcome:
I act faster and smarter.

Reflection

Where am I over-relying on data without trusting instinct?

Where am I ignoring data that could sharpen me

How can I merge both for stronger decisions?

WORKBOOK EXERCISE: BALANCE CHECK

Step 1: Identify three decisions ahead of me.
Decision 1 →
Decision 2 →
Decision 3 →

Step 2: For each, ask:
What does the data say?

What does instinct say?

Step 3: Write my "Balanced Move" for each decision.
  Decision 1 → (e.g., confirm with numbers, decide with gut)

  Decision 2 → (e.g., trust patterns but lean on vision)

  Decision 3 → (e.g., use both inputs for clarity)

Decision Filter Questions
  Is this data-informed but not data-defined?
  Does instinct sharpen this decision?
  Would combining both give me the edge?

This Week, I Will Balance Data And Instinct By:

PRINCIPLE #94

KNOW THE COST OF SAYING YES

The Core Idea:
Every yes is a no to something else.

Why It Matters:
Every yes has a price.

How It Helps:
I calculate opportunity cost.

The Outcome:
I protect my priorities.

Reflection

What yeses have cost me more than I realized?

Where am I saying yes too cheaply?

What would change if I valued my focus like currency?

WORKBOOK EXERCISE: YES COSTING

Step 1: Identify three recent or upcoming yeses.
Yes 1 →
Yes 2 →
Yes 3 →

Step 2: For each, ask:
What did this yes cost?

Was it worth it?

Step 3: Write my "Wise Yes Move" for each.

Yes 1 → (e.g., decline or renegotiate)

Yes 2 → (e.g., align with top priorities)

Yes 3 → (e.g., free bandwidth by cutting elsewhere)

Decision Filter Questions

What no comes with this yes?
Is this worth the focus it costs?
Does this yes build or dilute me?

This Week, I Will Value My Yes By:

PRINCIPLE #95

OPERATE LIKE A FOUNDER, EVEN WHEN YOU'RE NOT

The Core Idea:
I treat every job, project, and opportunity like my name's on it.

Why It Matters:
Ownership is mindset before title.

How It Helps:
I take extreme responsibility.

The Outcome:
I earn leadership by behavior.

Reflection

Where am I acting like a passenger instead of a founder?

How would things change if I treated this like it was mine?

What behaviors would make me the obvious leader here?

WORKBOOK EXERCISE: FOUNDER'S LENS

Step 1: Identify three areas where I don't feel like the owner.
Work →
Relationships →
Projects →

Step 2: For each, ask:
What would an owner do here?

How do I step into responsibility?

Step 3: Write my "Score Move" for each area.

Business → (e.g., measure revenue milestones privately)

Health → (e.g., log training consistency)

Personal Growth → (e.g., journal progress, not announce it)

Decision Filter Questions

Am I keeping score quietly?
Do I know if I'm winning or just moving?
Would tracking sharpen discipline here?

This Week, I Will Keep Score Quietly By:

PRINCIPLE #97

BUILD A LIFE YOU DON'T NEED A VACATION FROM

The Core Idea:
Escape isn't the goal. Alignment is.

Why It Matters:
Escaping isn't living.

How It Helps:
I align work with values.

The Outcome:
I find peace in the process.

Reflection

Where do I crave escape more than I enjoy alignment?

What would life look like if every day felt chosen?

How could I integrate joy into my daily rhythm?

WORKBOOK EXERCISE: ALIGNMENT BUILDER

Step 1: Identify three areas I often want to escape from.
Work →
Health →
Relationships →

Step 2: For each, ask:
Why do I want to escape this?

How can I realign it with my values?

Step 3: Write my "Alignment Move" for each area.

Work → (e.g., restructure for joy and freedom)

Health → (e.g., make routines enjoyable, not painful)

Relationships → (e.g., pursue alignment, not obligation)

Decision Filter Questions

Would I still choose this if I didn't need escape?
Am I aligned or escaping?
Does this life need vacations or does it feel whole?

This Week, I Will Design Life For Alignment By:

PRINCIPLE #98

AVOID ANYTHING THAT COMPLICATES YOUR PEACE

The Core Idea:
Peace is leverage. I won't trade it for vanity or validation.

Why It Matters:
Peace is the rarest currency.

How It Helps:
I cut chaos, even if it's profitable.

The Outcome:
I gain margin to think and thrive.

Reflection

Where am I trading peace for profit or appearances?

What chaos am I tolerating that I could cut?

How has protecting peace sharpened me in the past?

WORKBOOK EXERCISE: PEACE AUDIT

Step 1: Identify three areas that disrupt my peace.
Work →
Relationships →
Lifestyle →

Step 2: For each, ask:
Is this worth the cost of peace?

How could I simplify or exit?

Step 3: Write my "Peace Move" for each area.

Work → (e.g., decline misaligned deals)

Relationships → (e.g., set boundaries, reduce drama)

Lifestyle → (e.g., simplify commitments, remove vanity noise)

Decision Filter Questions

Does this protect or complicate my peace?
Am I trading peace for profit or validation?
Would simpler give me more leverage?

This Week, I Will Protect My Peace By:

PRINCIPLE #99

BE YOUR OWN SAFETY NET

The Core Idea:
I don't wait for rescue. I build resilience from the inside out.

Why It Matters:
Self-reliance scales security.

How It Helps:
I stack resources, skills, and systems.

The Outcome:
I stay grounded when others shake.

Reflection

Where am I dependent on others for stability?

What skills or reserves would make me resilient?

How can I create systems that protect me in storms?

WORKBOOK EXERCISE: RESILIENCE BUILDER

Step 1: Identify three pillars of your personal safety net.
Cash Reserves →
Skills/Income Streams →
Systems/Support →

Step 2: For each, ask:
What's my current strength here?

What's missing?

Step 3: Write my "Safety Net Move" for each pillar.
Cash Reserves → (e.g., build 6–12 months runway)

Skills/Income Streams → (e.g., add a durable secondary skill)

Systems/Support → (e.g., create contingency plans and backups)

Decision Filter Questions

Would I be okay if external support vanished?
What redundancy protects me here?
Am I building true resilience or hoping for rescue?

This Week, I Will Strengthen My Safety Net By:

PRINCIPLE #100

DIE WITH NOTHING LEFT UNKNOWN

The Core Idea:
When I leave, I leave it all on the field. Every idea. Every gift. Every bit of impact I was meant to give.

Why It Matters:
Potential unused is purpose wasted.

How It Helps:
I create, share, build, and give until the end.

The Outcome:
I leave nothing on the table, and no one wondering what I could've been.

Reflection

What vision, work, or love am I still holding back?

If today were my last day, what would I regret not giving?

How can I live each week with nothing withheld?

WORKBOOK EXERCISE: LEAVE IT ALL

Step 1: Identify three gifts or ideas I'm still holding.
Gift/Idea 1 →
Gift/Idea 2 →
Gift/Idea 3 →

Step 2: For each, ask:
What's stopping me from giving this now?

What's the smallest action that puts it into the world?

Step 3: Write my "Nothing Left Move" for each.

Gift/Idea 1 → (e.g., publish, ship, or share this week)

Gift/Idea 2 → (e.g., mentor or teach someone now)

Gift/Idea 3 → (e.g., start the project and set a stake)

Decision Filter Questions

Am I leaving anything unlived?
What am I still withholding that the world needs?
If not now, when?

This Week, I Will Leave Nothing On The Table By:

REFLECTIONS ON THE COMPASS

You've walked through one hundred principles. Not as slogans. Not as motivational fluff. But as systems: tested, explained, and translated into practice.

If you've done the work, asked the questions, written the answers, tried the exercises; you now hold more than pages. You hold proof. Proof that alignment can be designed. That peace can be protected. That freedom, mastery, and legacy are not accidents but outcomes.

But here's the truth: you are not finished. Principles are not something you "check off." They are compasses: tools you return to, filters you revisit, anchors you test against new winds and new seasons. What they mean today will not be what they mean a year from now. Growth changes the questions. But the compass keeps pointing north.

This section was about internal alignment: about building the roots. The next section is about external decisions: protecting that alignment when pressure rises.

Closing Exercise: Alignment Review
Step 1: List the five principles that hit you the hardest.
1.
2.
3.
4.
5.

Step 2: For each, ask:
Why did this resonate?

What misalignment did it expose?

What action does it demand now?

Step 3: Write your "Top Alignment Move" for the next 30 days.

Step 4: Out of the 5 principles you listed in Step 1, circle one principle... the one you're committing to fully live out this month, "no excuses."

Principles only matter when they are lived. Don't just carry them in your head; carry them into your habits, your calendar, your conversations, your commitments.

You now hold 100 principles, not as quotes to admire, but as frameworks to live.

You've seen why they matter, how they work, and what they unlock when practiced with discipline.

More importantly, you've translated them into action.

Alignment only matters if it shows up in your decisions.

And that's where we go next.

SECTION III

86 DECISION QUESTIONS TO GUIDE THE CLIMB

The filters I use to decide what moves forward, what gets built, and what gets left behind.

Principles are the foundation. Reflections are the practice. But in the end, alignment is proven at the point of decision.

That's what this section is for: questions. Not vague, feel-good questions, but sharp filters that cut through noise. Questions that protect clarity when emotions are high, when momentum is deceptive, or when success starts to create as much distraction as failure.

Every major choice I make runs through these filters. If it fails the test, it doesn't move forward. Period.

Here's what these questions do:

They slow me down when the rush would cost me.

They expose the hidden tradeoffs in every "yes."

They keep my decisions aligned with peace, purpose, mastery, freedom, and legacy.

Where Section II built roots, Section III builds guardrails. These are the checks that keep the compass steady when the climb gets steep.

Turn the page and begin. Ask the questions. Let them do their work. If the answer exposes drift, it's better to find it here than after the fall.

1. **Does this create ownership or dependency?**
    Intent: I want to build what empowers me long-term, not what makes me reliant on others.

2. **Is this aligned with my long-term purpose or just feeding the moment?**
    Intent: Temporary satisfaction can derail strategic direction.

3. **Would I still choose this if no one ever found out I did it?**
    Intent: I'm testing for intrinsic motivation over optics.

4. **Is this scalable, or is it built on my burnout?**
    Intent: Sustainability beats speed. I avoid models that depend on exhaustion.

5. **Will this still matter in 10 years?**
    Intent: Longevity reveals what truly matters.

6. **Does this move me toward peace or further into pressure?**
    Intent: Peace is my compass, not just productivity.

7. **Am I saying yes because I want to or because I'm afraid to say no?**
    Intent: Fear-based decisions lead to misalignment.

8. **Does this multiply my time, energy, or capacity?**
    Intent: I'm seeking leverage, not load.

9.   **Is this something only I can do, or am I preventing someone else's growth?**
     Intent: Delegation is how I scale and empower others.

10. **Am I solving a real problem or creating one?**
     Intent: I want to eliminate friction, not build work for work's sake.

11. **Would I be proud if this showed up on the front page?**
     Intent: Reputation is built in private, tested in public.

12. **Is this driven by values or vanity?**
     Intent: Integrity must guide direction, not ego.

13. **Am I rushing this because of pressure or clarity?**
     Intent: Urgency without clarity creates mistakes.

14. **Would my future self thank me or resent me for this?**
     Intent: I'm playing the long game, not just today's game.

15. **Does this keep me in integrity with who I say I am?**
     Intent: Consistency between my word and action builds self-trust.

16. **Am I building leverage or building noise?**
     Intent: I want compounding impact, not hollow output.

17. **Would I do this if it never made a dollar?**
     Intent: Purpose outlasts profit.

18. **Is this me responding or reacting?**
     Intent: I act from intention, not emotion.

19. **Does this simplify or complicate my path?**
     Intent: Clarity accelerates execution.

20. **What's the cost of saying yes, and what's the cost of saying no?**
     Intent: Every choice has an unseen tradeoff.

21. **Is this a detour or a distraction?**
     Intent: Not all side paths are strategic.

22. **What part of this am I avoiding looking at honestly?**
     Intent: Avoidance always creates future consequences.

23. **Does this create dependency on others, or resilience in me?**
     Intent: Resilience is the foundation of freedom.

24. **Is this addition or subtraction to the mission?**
     Intent: I filter for alignment, not accumulation.

25. **Am I choosing this out of love or fear?**
    Intent: I want decisions rooted in conviction, not survival.

26. **Who benefits from this... really?**
    Intent: Hidden agendas cloud impact.

27. **Is this a short-term fix or a long-term shift?**
    Intent: I want transformation, not patches.

28. **Am I confusing motion with progress?**
    Intent: Activity ≠ achievement.

29. **Does this keep the promise I made to myself?**
    Intent: Self-respect is earned through consistency.

30. **Is this me solving the problem... or avoiding the deeper one?**
    Intent: I want to treat root cause, not surface symptoms.

31. **Have I counted the hidden costs?**
    Intent: True ROI includes the invisible toll.

32. **Does this preserve the culture I'm building?**
    Intent: Culture compounds through every choice.

33. **If this fails, will I be okay with the reason why?**
    Intent: I'm okay with risk, not with compromise.

34. **Would I advise my closest friend to do this?**
    Intent: External perspective reveals hidden truths.

35. **Am I honoring my rhythm or forcing a cycle I've outgrown?**
    Intent: Growth requires updated timing.

36. **Do I feel lighter or heavier when I think about this?**
    Intent: My body knows what my mind hides.

37. **Is this a door I opened, or one I'm forcing?**
    Intent: Flow feels different from force.

38. **Is the ROI emotional, spiritual, financial... or just busywork?**
    Intent: I want returns that matter.

39. **Am I trying to prove something, or build something?**
    Intent: Insecurity creates distractions.

40. **If I lost everything tomorrow, would I regret doing this?**
    Intent: Regret-proof decisions are built on purpose.

41. **Is this the next right step, or just the next available one?**
    Intent: I want intentional action, not default reaction.

42. **Does this honor the season I'm in?**
    Intent: Every season requires different stewardship.

43. **Who do I become if I say yes to this?**
    Intent: Identity is shaped by agreement.

44. **Have I already outgrown this idea?**
    Intent: Not all good ideas are still right.

45. **Am I doing this from abundance or scarcity?**
    Intent: Scarcity-based moves limit growth.

46. **What pattern is this continuing or breaking?**
    Intent: I lead cycles, not relive them.

47. **Am I investing in something that will invest back?**
    Intent: I want energy to return, not drain.

48. **Does this deepen my mastery or distract from it?**
    Intent: Excellence requires discipline.

49. **Is this the hard thing that matters or just hard for the sake of hard?**
    Intent: Difficulty ≠ value.

50. **What would I need to let go of to fully commit to this?**
    Intent: Focus requires sacrifice.

51. **Am I honoring my boundaries or betraying them?**
    Intent: Saying yes without limits builds resentment.

52. **What am I afraid will happen if I don't do this?**
    Intent: Fear reveals my attachments.

53. **Will this matter when I look back on my life?**
    Intent: Legacy filters urgency.

54. **Is this rooted in who I really am or who I'm trying to be?**
    Intent: Authenticity must lead strategy.

55. **What friction is here and what is it trying to teach me?**
    Intent: Resistance reveals refinement.

56. **Will this increase or erode trust with my team?**
    Intent: Culture is fragile and contagious.

57. **What would I do if I knew this would succeed?**
Intent: Fear shouldn't decide scale.

58. **What would I do if I knew it could fail... and be worth it anyway?**
Intent: Some risks are worth the lesson.

59. **Am I taking the easy path or the aligned one?**
Intent: Ease and alignment aren't the same.

60. **Have I given this the attention it deserves, or am I just reacting?**
Intent: Attention reveals value.

61. **What version of me is making this decision... the healed one or the hurt one?**
Intent: Unhealed decisions replicate old damage.

62. **If this works, does it create momentum or maintenance?**
Intent: I want to build compounding systems.

63. **If I couldn't talk about this, would I still want to do it?**
Intent: Quiet conviction beats loud ambition.

64. **Am I building for applause or for impact?**
Intent: Optics fade, outcomes last.

65. **Is this a mission, or a marketing plan?**
Intent: I want substance before spotlight.

66. **Am I being pulled toward this or pushing into it?**
Intent: Pull reveals alignment, push reveals pressure.

67. **If I knew I only had one year left, would I pursue this?**
Intent: Mortality clarifies priority.

68. **Am I living inside my design, or someone else's expectation?**
Intent: I lead from my blueprint, not their blueprint.

69. **Will this help someone else build their future, or just borrow mine?**
Intent: I want to create platforms, not crutches.

70. **Is this decision worthy of the sacrifice it will demand?**
Intent: Every yes costs something... it better be worth it.

71. **Have I built a runway for this, or just jumped into the air?**
Intent: Preparation enables sustainable flight.

72. **Does this build my story or distract from it?**
Intent: Every action writes my legacy.

73. **What's the truth I've been avoiding here?**
Intent: Unspoken truth is a silent saboteur.

74. **Is this creating leverage or locking me in?**
Intent: I want freedom baked into every frame.

75. **Have I talked myself into this, or out of what I actually want?**
Intent: Logic shouldn't override alignment.

76. **Am I being courageous or just compulsive?**
Intent: Intentional risk ≠ reactive action.

77. **What would this look like if it were easy?**
Intent: I remove unnecessary friction.

78. **What would this look like if it were clean?**
Intent: Simplicity reveals the truth.

79. **What would I do differently if I trusted myself more?**
Intent: Confidence sharpens decision quality.

80. **Who am I becoming through this... and is that someone I want to be?**
Intent: Becoming matters more than achieving.

81. **If this cost me everything... would it still be worth it?**
Intent: I only bet on things that matter that much.

82. **Will this still work if I'm gone for six months?**
Intent: Systems must survive without me.

83. **Am I building something that depends on me, or transcends me?**
Intent: Legacy means designing for independence.

84. **What would it take to design myself out of this system and still have it win?**
Intent: My goal is to lead something that doesn't need my constant presence.

85. **Will this make my son proud of me, or would I be proud to tell him about it and include him in it?**
Intent: I want to make decisions I'd be proud to share with the next generation, the kind that invite legacy, not secrecy.

86. **Is this worth the time away from the important things in my life... like family?**
Intent: Time is my most valuable asset, and I only spend it where it counts most.

THE COMPASS IS YOURS

You've walked the path.

The principles.

The reflections.

The questions.

You've wrestled with them, written through them, and tested them against your own story.

What you hold now is more than a book... it is a complete compass.

- Principles: the laws that govern the climb.
- Reflections: the practice that aligns belief with action.
- Decision Questions: the filters that protect clarity when the stakes rise.

This book does not hand you answers.

It gives you something far more powerful: alignment.

Because the truth is, the answers you're looking for are already inside you. The Compass is what keeps them pointed north, even when the terrain shifts or the winds turn against you.

The climb ahead will not get easier.

The noise around you will not get quieter.

The world will not suddenly clear a path for you.

But you will change.

You will get stronger, sharper, clearer, and more deeply rooted each time you return to these pages, not because the pages grow, but because you do. Every pass through the Compass carves the principles deeper into you until they are not just things you believe, but ways you live.

And when you face the next turning point, the decision that could shift your life, your business, your legacy, remember the truths that outlast pressure:

- If it builds ownership, choose it.
- If it creates peace, protect it.
- If it compounds over time, commit to it.
- If it honors who you truly are, stand by it.
- And if it will still matter when you're gone, give it everything.

Because the world does not need more people chasing noise. It does not need more lives scattered by distraction or more leaders hollowed out by compromise.

What it needs are men and women who live aligned.

Builders who think in decades, not days.

Visionaries who leave nothing undone, who choose roots over applause, who plant what will outlast them.

That is the invitation.

Not to finish this book, but to live it.

Not to admire the Compass, but to carry it.

Not to keep it as a private tool, but to embody it so fully that others can follow your life with trust.

The Compass is yours now. Hold it. Use it. Test it against every new season, every new decision, every new challenge. Let it remind you that clarity is possible, that peace can be protected, and that your future is not a matter of chance, it is a matter of choice.

You hold the Compass. The direction is yours to set.

A Final Note from the Author

None of this came easy.

None of it is hypothetical.

These words carry the weight of blood, sweat, mistakes, lessons, and the quiet work of getting back up when I wanted to stay down. They are the scaffolding I built when I had no map, the compass I tested in real storms.

If you take one thing from this book, let it be this:
Your Life Is Too Valuable To Drift.

Drift may feel easier in the moment, but it always extracts a price, your peace, your purpose, your time, your freedom. Alignment is not a luxury reserved for the lucky or the disciplined. Alignment is survival. It is the only way to climb without breaking under pressure, the only way to move forward with clarity instead of chaos.

I don't know what mountain you're standing at the base of right now. Maybe it's financial. Maybe it's relational. Maybe it's a vision that feels too heavy to carry or too distant to believe in. But I do know this: with clarity, conviction, and the courage to live aligned and architect your future, you can climb it. Not quickly. Not without struggle. But steadily, step by step, with roots that hold and direction that does not waver.

And here is the greater truth:
The Summit Is Not The End Of The Story.

The climb is not just about reaching the top, it's about what you build once you are there. Because reaching the summit without peace is hollow. Achieving success without alignment is fragile.

The goal is not just to win, but to build something that lasts, something that carries weight beyond your lifetime. Legacy is not found at the peak, it is forged along the climb and solidified in what you leave behind.

So let this not be the end, but a turning point. These pages are finished, but your work is not.

It is your turn now: to live aligned, to guard what matters most, to protect your peace even when the world pushes against it, and to build your legacy one aligned decision at a time.

Because your future is not an accident. It will be the outcome of what you choose to live by.

Live aligned.

Protect your peace.

Build your legacy.

Own The Future.

– KL Renner

AFTERWORD

COMPASS STATEMENT

Every climb is personal. Every compass points true north, but the path is yours to walk.

As you close this book, take a moment to write down the essence of your compass; what you want to carry forward, return to, and be known for.

MY COMPASS STATEMENT

The principle I will live by:

The peace I will protect:

The purpose I will pursue:

The legacy I will leave:

This is your north star. Write it honestly. Revisit it often. Live it daily.
The compass is yours now.
Go Clim

OWN THE FUTURE

**A MASTER GUIDE TO LIVING,
LEADING, AND DECIDING WITH
INTEGRITY AND IMPACT**

www.ingramcontent.com/pod-product-compliance
Lightning Source LLC
Chambersburg PA
CBHW060416130626
46555CB00005B/2092